HAITI

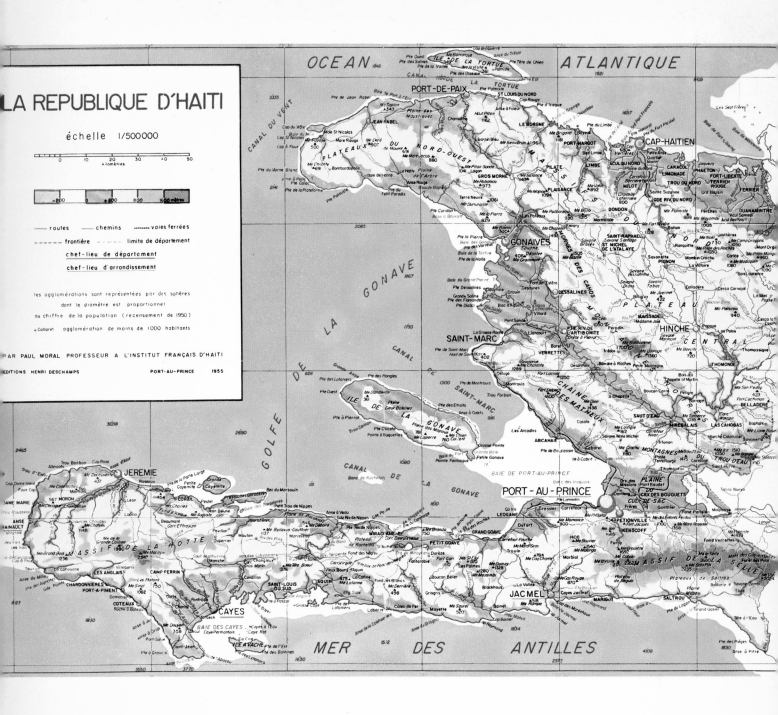

LA REPUBLIQUE D'HAITI

échelle 1/500000

kilomètres

- routes — chemins ····· voies ferrées
- - - - - frontière - · - · - limite de département

chef-lieu de département

chef-lieu d'arrondissement

les agglomérations sont représentées par des sphères
dont le diamètre est proportionnel
au chiffre de la population (recensement de 1950)

• Cabaret agglomération de moins de 1000 habitants

PAR PAUL MORAL PROFESSEUR A L'INSTITUT FRANÇAIS D'HAITI

EDITIONS HENRI DESCHAMPS   PORT-AU-PRINCE   1955

ALFRED MÉTRAUX

HAITI

BLACK PEASANTS
AND VOODOO

PHOTOGRAPHS BY

PIERRE VERGER AND ALFRED MÉTRAUX

Translated from the French by

PETER LENGYEL

UNIVERSE BOOKS, PUBLISHERS, NEW YORK

The publishers wish to thank the following for their kind permission to reproduce certain plates:

Editions Henri Deschamps, Port-au-Prince: La République d'Haïti, *frontispiece map.*

National Tourist Office, Haiti: King Christophe's Tomb, pages 20-21.

Pan American World Airways: King Christophe's Citadel, between pages 22 and 23.

Coll. Claude Lévy-Strauss, Paris: Feasting Scene, by A. Lusimond, between pages 38 and 39.

I wish here to express my gratitude to all those who have helped me in my research:
M. Remy Bastien, M. E. Berrouet, M. and Mme Jean Comhaire-Sylvain,
M. Lamartinière Honorat, M. Michelson Paul Hyppolite and Mlle Jeanne G. Sylvain.

A. M.

First American Edition

L. C. Catalogue Card Number: 60-8172

© EDITION DE LA BACONNIÈRE 1960

PRINTED IN SWITZERLAND

Only one aspect of Haiti is discussed in this book, which deals with the *mornes*[1] and their inhabitants, which is to say the three million people living in the valleys and on the slopes of the mountains. The only urban scenes described picture that popular life which spills over generously into the towns from the surrounding countryside.

Many of my Haitian friends will regret a limitation which neglects features of their island in which they take pride and which they would like to have more widely known. In apologizing to them, I would also like to remind them that I was brought to their country to study rural life, and that an international organization gave me the task of laying the foundations of a fundamental education project there. Many of the details scattered throughout the following pages and concerning peasant life are based on my observations during a long stay in the Marbial valley. Sometimes they reflect local living conditions, but for the most part they apply to the country as a whole. Like all those who have visited Haiti, I have been won over by the charm of the peasants, by their friendliness, their gentleness and their hospitality. I was touched by their misery and shall always regret my inability to extend the help expected from me. During my time in Haiti, I was particularly occupied with voodoo, which gave me the chance to observe a rich and complex religion in many respects reminiscent of the pagan cults of Antiquity. I have thought it useful to reproduce some examples characteristic of the spoken language of the vast majority of Haitian people. " Creole " is not a kind of pidgin but the last-born of the Romance languages, derived from French in the same manner as French itself is derived from Latin. Though the vocabulary, with the exception of a certain number of terms of African or Spanish origin, is almost entirely French, the pronunciation and grammar bear the imprint of various West African languages. Professor Paul Zumthor, a Swiss Romance scholar, writes of Creole that " . . . it is of exceptional richness, ingenuity and colorfulness ; thousands of turns of speech can be quoted which, for their flavor and expressiveness as well as for their psychological, emotional and poetic content, are really unique. . . ." In order to underline the affinity between Creole and French, the Haitians spell their tongue in a capricious manner which tends to corrupt its pronunciation, giving it a false air of childish jargon. Following the example of linguists, I have preferred to use a simple phonetic transcription, identifying each sound by a distinct sign. I have abandoned this practice, however, for " ch " and " ou ", which represent the same sound as in French. Nasalization is indicated by a circumflex accent, as : ê.

Monsieur Pierre Verger, who has taken most of the snapshots illustrating this volume, is himself the author of *Dieux d'Afrique*, a book in which he has shown, in photographs, the persistence of African cults in Brazil. He combines his talents as a cameraman with a profound knowledge of the American Negroes and their cousins in Dahomey and Nigeria. Few ethnographers can claim to have plumbed so deeply the secrets of African societies in the Old World and the New.

---

[1] Hills in the West Indies.

CONTENTS

INTRODUCTION

Whether considered in time or space, Haiti is an island of many contrasts. A country of steep mountains and deep valleys, it contrasts lush plains with spiky deserts, limpid brooks with furious torrents ; the cold mist of the peaks with the humid heat of the plantations. Despite a modernizing drive, the old-time charm of former ports of call hangs over its coastal cities.

In less than four centuries, the country has been known as Haiti, Hispaniola, Santo Domingo and then Haiti again when its inhabitants wished to emphasize their break away from Europe. Three races have succeeded each other on its territory : it was the home of Indian tribes from Amazonas, the promised land of the first Spanish settlers, the haunt of pirates, the richest colony of the kingdom of France and, lastly, the world's first black republic. For over a century and a half, Haiti's destiny has been alternately in the hands of emperors, kings, dictators, and presidents. It is proud to have been the home of Toussaint L'Ouverture, one of the most noble figures in American history, but ashamed of the rule of ignorant and temperamental tyrants.

From the dawn of its history, mulattoes and Negroes have faced each other with hate in their hearts. To the present day, its population is deeply divided and its upper class has been referred to as a " caste." The term is misleading, but it is nevertheless true that a profound schism exists between a light colored minority (including a few Negro families), which considers itself to be the chosen élite and sticks desperately to Western ways of life

and thought, and the rural masses, black-skinned, crinkly-haired, still maintaining many links with ancestral Africa and living poorly on divided and decreasingly fertile lands.

Of all the aspects of Haiti, this essay intends to deal precisely with the one which is a source of distress to many Haitians and which, quite mistakenly, they wish to conceal.

Since the island has become a tourist attraction, albums extolling its beauty abound : they show the luxurious villas of Petionville against a background of mountains, modern hotels set among palms and mango trees, coral reefs suitable for underwater fishing and girls with complexions so fair that they might be taken for Italians. If the " common people " are remembered at all, it is to provide an element of the picturesque ; they are represented by a " merry peasant " astride an ass or by young ladies giving a performance in national costumes. In one such work, the author, overcome by scruples, wanted to pay tribute to the tiller of the soil. He included a picture of him, but this peasant who symbolizes 98% of Haiti's population is seen from behind, so that, in his rough blue smock, he might well be taken for a Norman. It is this picture which induced me to write a book in which the inhabitant of the *mornes* might be seen full face.

His very black face is indeed a picture of goodness and wisdom. In the past two centuries, he has seen trials sufficient to break the toughest character. He has been " piece of the Indies, " slave, insurgent, a soldier in civil wars, but through all these vicissitudes he has remained a peasant. He is attached to this soil to which his ancestors were deported with the single-minded passion binding a European peasant to a plot cultivated for thousands of years. He is a simple, stubborn and grasping peasant, but also courteous, gay and the guardian of artistic traditions lost to the West. By describing his work and his days, by making known his beliefs, I wish to acknowledge my debt to the soil of Haiti, which made me so warmly welcome.

THE BIRTH OF HAITI AS A NATION

Much has changed in Haiti since December 6, 1492, when Christopher Columbus, on board the *Santa Maria*, described the coast and the people he had just discovered :

" The following day, he [Christopher Columbus] landed nine well-armed men who, after advancing four leagues, came upon a village consisting of some thousand houses scattered in a valley. As soon as they caught sight of the Christians, the Indians abandoned the village and fled into the forest ; but the Indian guide from San Salvador, whom our men had brought along, followed them and, by calling out and telling them about the Christians who, he said, were come from Heaven, made them return calm and confident. Later, filled with awe and wonderment, they put their hands on the heads of our men as if to honor them ; they brought them victuals, giving them all they could find and asking nothing in return, and begged them to spend the night in their village ; but the Christians did not wish to accept without first returning to their ship to impart how pleasant they had found the land, how abundant the food and that the people were much whiter and of greater beauty than those they had come across on other isles, being also docile and forthcoming." (Fernando Colón, *Historia del Almirante de Las Indias Don Cristobal Colón*, Chapter XXX.)

The charming Taino Indians, whose villages were strung out along the coast, had disappeared to the last man within less than a century. The only surviving reminders of their former presence are some mysterious designs carved in the rocks, a few rotting skeletons in caves and, on the ancient village sites, innumerable potsherds decorated with strange figures which the black peasants call " the eyes of the earth." In glades and clearings they also left marvellous stone axes, so smooth and glossy that one could never tire of stroking them. Before they became extinct, the Tainos bequeathed to their successors their knowledge of edible plants, such as maize, manioc and sweet potatoes, on which the latter-day peasants still feed. Thus the sons of Africa perpetuate the economy of a people whose very existence they never suspect.

The extermination of the Tainos is one of the episodes in the conquest of the New World which the vehement denunciations of Las Casas have made famous. It would have been altogether healthier for the subsequent glory of this champion of the Indians had he not sanctioned the introduction of African slaves to take the place of his protégés, but it is incorrect to maintain that he was actually responsible for the trade which was to take on such proportions and which he himself deplored. African slaves are known to have been in Haiti by 1510, and during the 16th century some of them had run away and were fighting for their liberty.

The birth of the French colony of Santo Domingo was made possible when Spanish settlers abandoned a large part of Haiti, finding Mexico and Peru more attractive, and later through the relentless wars waged by the French, the English and the Dutch against the Spaniards. Around 1626, the island of La Tortue, to the north of Haiti, had become the meeting place of pirates, while buccaneers, in search of wild pigs and cattle, roamed the nearby mainland, by then again a primitive wilderness.

Thanks to such adventurers, France was able to gain a foothold in Haiti, and by the beginning of the 18th century, Santo Domingo became a source of immense riches. The colony was to the national economy of France what India was to become to that of England. To raise the sugar cane, on which prosperity was based, called for an abundant supply of labor. This came from Africa. Santo Domingo became one of the apexes of that triangular route which took the vessels from Nantes or Bordeaux to the African coast, where they loaded their cargo of " ebony " to be traded in Santo Domingo for sugar, which the same ships then brought back to their home ports. The fine town houses of Nantes and Bordeaux remain as monuments to the profitability of such commerce.

Seeing a list of the tribes represented in Santo Domingo could induce one to believe that the ancestors of the Haitian people came from all over Africa, but in fact, though the work gangs were composed of the most diverse elements, the majority of the captives originated from that African region long known as the Slave Coast. The treaty ports of Dahomey and Nigeria supplied the largest contingents of " ebony." The history of the trade, the evidence adduced by bills of lading of the Negro vessels and by certificates of sale, suffices to indicate the size of the Dahomeyan element in the slave population. Over two centuries of total separation from Africa, moreover, have not wiped out all traces of Dahomey ; they are still sufficiently marked to be identified in a thousand details of everyday life, even if all historical evidence had been lost. The great conquerors who built the empire of Dahomey were suppliers to French and Portuguese planters. The town of Ouidah in Dahomey was one of Africa's largest slave markets right down to the middle of last century. When one crosses the seven miles of marsh and dune which lie between Ouidah and the sea, one cannot help remembering those thousands of men, women and children for whom this was the last lap of their journey and the final break with the continent

of their birth. The memory of so much misery still weighs on the desolate countryside and on the beach from which they all left.

That the fate of the slaves in Haiti was, after all, a better one than that which would have awaited them had they stayed in Africa was a common 18th-century argument designed to appease consciences, and is still heard occasionally. In contrast to the idyllic accounts of plantation life which have been written, the following description by a Swiss who visited Haiti shortly before the French Revolution may be set :

" There were about a hundred men and women of all ages working to dig ditches in a cane field, the majority of them naked or dressed in rags. The sun beat down on their heads ; sweat ran from every part of their bodies. Their limbs were numbed by the heat, tired out by the weight of heavy picks and by the difficulty of moving soil loamy and hard enough to break the very tools ; yet they strained to overcome all hindrances. Dismal silence reigned among them, suffering was etched on every face, but the hour of rest had not yet come. The gang was under the unmerciful eye of the overseer, and several drivers armed with long whips were scattered among the workers, and from time to time indiscriminately lashed those who, overcome by weariness, seemed forced to slow down, whether they were Negroes or Negresses, young or old."

The atrocities committed on the plantations might seem incredible if Europeans themselves had not, in turn, fallen victim to the same practices under totalitarian regimes. Negroes whipped to death, burned and buried alive, fed to the ants—the story of their sufferings and of the bloodthirsty fury of their masters was buried in the colonial files until scholars unearthed it. Good and generous slaveowners no doubt existed, but how heavily does their paternalistic care weigh in the balance against a monstrous system ? Neither historical nor æsthetic romanticism can veil the plain facts. Weakened by overwork, undernourished and ill-treated, the slave population of Santo Domingo multiplied slowly or not at all. It was constantly necessary to raid Africa to keep up the island's supply of labor. Every year, thousands of blacks transported in the Negro ships came to take the place of those whom the soil of Haiti had swallowed. How much has been said and written about the servile spirit and patient resignation of the Negro ! But the hate which lay in their hearts and their fierce love of liberty never ceased to find expression in flight and revolt. Even during the most prosperous period, the Haitian *mornes* were bastions of embittered freedom. Thousands of runaway Negroes and Negresses hid in the Selle mountains and fought desperately against the troops sent to pursue them. These outcasts knew how to find their leaders : one of them, Makandal, had the idea of liquidating the entire white population long before the revolution occurred to shake Santo Domingo. Out of the hate engendered by local uprisings, out of the cruelty of repression and the misery of the entire people, the independence of Haiti was born. The French Revolution gave all these ambitions and all this hate a chance to crystallize into a revolt which, after fifteen years of fighting, made Haiti a free country. The great storm which was to break over Santo Domingo was heralded and kindled by the antagonism which,

after 1790, set the plantation owners against the " poor whites " and the mulattoes. Colored people bitterly demanded that equality which the Constituent Assembly had proclaimed, but which the white settlers held back from them. Of the blacks there was no mention at all, and the idea of abolishing slavery long remained as foreign to the mulattoes as to the whites. Haiti would have remained a French colony, like Guadeloupe or Martinique, and slavery would not have been abolished there for another fifty years if, in 1791, the blacks in the gangs had not suddenly risen and won their liberty at the cost of their blood.

According to a carefully preserved tradition, the revolt was decided upon during the night of August 14, 1791, on the Turpin homestead. At the behest of one Boukman, a sort of giant who was also a voodoo priest, the slaves of the plantation met in a clearing of the Caiman woods, near the Morne Rouge. A hurricane on that night added to the drama of the scene. An old Negress with a knife in her hand rose, her body shaking. Amid universal silence, she plunged the knife into the throat of a black pig. Its blood, caught in a gourd, was passed from hand to hand. All those who drank of it swore to obey Boukman . . . On the night of August 22, flames rose from all the plantations. The merciless civil war thus begun dragged on for a dozen years. So crazy and blind an uprising would have been but a peasant revolt, easily put down, if there had not emerged from the rabble of slaves leaders who knew how to command and how to organize, like Toussaint L'Ouverture, Dessalines and Christophe. Though Toussaint L'Ouverture, a victim of Bonaparte's perfidy, ultimately died in a dungeon of the fortress of Joux, near the Swiss border, his generals Dessalines and Christophe, supported by the mulatto general Pétion, destroyed the French troops sent out by the First Consul. On January 1, 1804, Dessalines proclaimed the independence of Haiti. A wholesale massacre obliterated the whites.

This liberty had been dearly purchased : for ten years, blood had not ceased to flow, nor buildings to burn. Dessalines summarized his strategy in a celebrated phrase : " *Boulé kay, coupé têt* " (" Burn the houses, cut off the heads ").

Napoleon's fundamental error was to despise the blacks and to underestimate Toussaint L'Ouverture. He admitted as much later and, on Saint Helena, reproached himself for having destroyed Toussaint, who had successfully restored the colony's prosperity, instead of winning him over and making him the island's governor. Attempting to reduce to slavery men who had fought so toughly to abolish it was a forlorn enterprise. Is it not unthinkable that General Dessalines, who bore the mark of the whip on his body, would accept a return to a social order which would have made human cattle again of his compatriots?

Victory, however, did not mean that the Haitian masses obtained complete freedom or gained immediate possession of the lands they so dearly coveted. Dessalines, having become Emperor, wished to hold the rural people to the soil by links which really constituted a system of serfdom; the only compensation he offered was relief from corporal punishment and a reduction in working hours. His assassination closed an era during which the military was well on the way to becoming the new class of feudal overlords, but King Christophe was hardly more liberal: decreeing in his turn that the tiller was forbidden to leave the soil of his birth, he also instituted a kind of serfdom. Furthermore, he imposed rigorous discipline on the peasants: laziness was an offence punishable by imprisonment or a sentence of hard labor. He tried to create a sort of aristocracy by distributing titles to his generals and favorites. Christophe's system collapsed with his death. Today, Haitians venerate the memory of this king who left a curious monument: the famous Citadel. Obsessed by the fear of a French return, he hit upon the idea of building an impregnable fortress. This impressive edifice, which was never put to any practical test, has been compared to the pyramids of the Pharaohs and dubbed "the eighth wonder of the world." It will never be known just how much sweat and blood it cost the people of Haiti to give this dream substance. The Citadel, rising from its peak like a black challenge to the whites, symbolizes King Christophe's determination, shared by the whole Haitian people, to remain free. As such, it is a national shrine to Haitians, referred to only with emotion and pride. President Pétion's more liberal policies favored the establishment of small holdings and a new Negro peasantry.

It is easy to be severe on the leaders who founded the State of Haiti. It is too readily forgotten that, with the exception of mulattoes like Pétion and Boyer, they were all former slaves without any political or administrative training, who shaped the exercise of their power on the only pattern familiar to them—that of the colony of Santo Domingo and the rebel army. For a long time, Haiti was nothing more than an isolated encampment in a perpetual state of emergency. The 1805 Constitution declares: "At the first shot of the warning cannon the towns will be razed and the nation will rise in arms." That gang and army discipline marked the political manners and outlook of the Haitians is therefore hardly surprising.

Military proclamations and civil wars are the stuff of Haitian history right down to the beginning of our century. Among the various heavy handed presidents who succeeded each other, Soulouque, who had himself proclaimed emperor under the name of Faustin the First, attracted European attention by the farcical pomp of his court.

The first fifty or sixty years of the republic were a period of isolation and stagnation. Reports by the few travelers who stayed on the island during this time make painful reading. Schœlcher, the liberator of the Negroes, saw the stagnation in which Haiti floundered as dangerous ammunition which the partisans of slavery might use against the abolitionists, but he notes nevertheless that, no matter how miserable, no peasant would barter his liberty for the comforts of even the most privileged slaves. The love of liberty equally fired the inhabitants of the *mornes* and the generals, thrown up as masters of the country by the accidents of a revolution.

The peasants participated only indirectly in the vicissitudes of Haitian politics. They became soldiers in that ill-assorted army which consumed half the national income, and grew the coffee which kept a desperate Treasury in funds. The government, whether controlled by semi-literate blacks or educated mulattoes, was largely indifferent to the peasant's fate : no serious attempt was made to look after his instruction or health and, until 1860, Haiti was in fact separated from the Roman Catholic Church. The Catholic clergy was locally represented only by adventurers ready for any kind of deal. It is therefore not surprising that the rites and beliefs of Africa crystallized into a semi-pagan religion —voodoo—to which the peasants remain strongly attached. One might almost say, quite unparadoxically, that it was voodoo which, by incorporating many Catholic practices, contributed towards the popular preservation of the Catholic tradition during the " great schism."

An important date in Haitian history is July 28, 1915. For on that day American marines landed to restore order after a period of bloodshed, and began an occupation which was to last for nineteen years. Haiti became a protectorate of the United States, almost a colony. Although the presence of American officials and garrisons of the marines was felt to be unspeakably humiliating by the entire Haitian middle class, the armed resistance of the peasants—the famous " cacos "—was fleeting. Haitians still refer to the American regime with resentment but, now that tempers have cooled, they admit that the outcome was at the end not entirely negative. Useful reforms were made and important public works initiated. The new era which thus opened for Haiti certainly did not put a stop to the revolutionary cycle. But such political upsets as accompanied the downfall of heads of state over the past twenty years have not shaken the country's structure as fundamentally as they did during the " time of the bayonets." Haiti seems at last to have found a certain stability which has allowed it to develop and to make appreciable progress in certain directions. The countryside is peaceful, and the peasants can till their land and go to market without having to fear conscription into some insurgent army. Educational extension and more constant contact with urban centers have somewhat modified the peasants' attitude to life. They have become more keenly aware of their precarious situation and aim to better their lot. This awakening is an important, perhaps even decisive, influence on the future of Haiti.

A sharp contrast often exists between the beauty of the Haitian landscape and the condition of the human beings who live against this delightful background. It is quite unnecessary to consult statistics or to know the size of the average family income in order to appreciate the peasant's poverty. Is not this sufficiently displayed by his patched and washed-out clothes, by his rickety home and by the nakedness of his potbellied children ? There are, of course, some well-off peasants, but the standards of comfort they enjoy would be considered rather modest elsewhere. The heavy liabilities of the past century are to a large extent responsible for present misery : isolation, economic depression, governmental indifference, civil wars, such are the factors which have held the peasant's progress in check, to which must be added ignorance and attachment to routine. All the liberated peasant had to fall back upon were enfeebled African traditions and what slight knowledge he might have picked up on the plantations. Until recently, no effort was made to get him out of these doldrums. Nevertheless, if this precarious situation had not had causes other than those which have just been listed, the highest hopes could be entertained. By correcting past errors, prosperity could have been made to return, but the evil lies deeper and is linked to a phenomenon against which it is hard to fight. The ruin of the peasants lies in the curse of excess population, which afflicts so many underdeveloped countries. Haiti is America's most densely populated region : there are 250 inhabitants to the square kilometer. In 150 years, the population has jumped from 400,000 to 3,100,000. At the beginning of the century, the Republic of Haiti occupied the whole of the island. Today, it is confined to a third of it. This already restricted area is mountainous, and 80% of the arable land is situated on the slopes of high mountains. Demographic pressure, barely relieved by a high rate of infant mortality, is illustrated by figures which alone sum up the tragedy of a land-hungry people. Property has been subdivided to such an extent that in certain regions which have been surveyed it is estimated that 80% of the peasants own under five hectares, 50% of whom possess less than one hectare and 25% less than half a hectare. Agricultural experts reckon at seven hectares the minimum off which a family can decently live.

With the exception of a few desert regions, the whole of Haiti, from the coastal plains to the highest mountains, is occupied. Peasants in search of land have erected their little huts and burned clearings in the forest wherever a corn cob or a yam will grow. Some even cultivate gardens on slopes so precipitous that it is said that they must rope themselves in order to weed them ! The diversity and broken up nature of the land, accidents of inheritance and of sales, have dispersed property, entailing difficulties and the extra effort which has to be put in by workers who are constantly on the move and cannot keep watch over their lands. This state of affairs has, to some extent, favored practical polygamy. It is in the interests of the owner of several scattered fields to install a " wife " on each of them who acts as a " steward "—a " garden-wife."

The subdivision and dispersion of landed property was aggravated with the years. Custom and law, without any regard for the ever-increasing population, decree that even the smallest plot of land be parcelled out at death to all the owner's children, whether legitimate or not. It is thus not uncommon for a hectare to be shared by six, eight or more persons. True, many inheritances stay in one piece to save the cost of surveying, but each portion is separately cultivated, and subdivision continues. Often that part which comes down to an individual is insignificant and is abandoned or sold, so that these strips of land, acquired by other peasants, are again split up.

Moreover, the fields are being constantly eaten into by the legal proceedings which the peasants institute against each other on trivial grounds, by the expense of surveying and, above all, by wasteful outlay on funerals. In every Haitian town and village there are lawyers and notaries who make fat profits out of the confused real estate situation which has always existed. A feeling of insecurity has developed in the peasant, due to the absence or dubious authenticity of title deeds and the fear of eviction : this flavors his stubborn attachment to the soil with bitterness. Land is to him not

only "his life" but also the source of dignity. Should he lose it, he is no more than a "vagabond" or "tramp"—a wandering and miserable creature fit only to rot in the slums of Port-au-Prince.

The plots, mercilessly exploited at the rate of two annual harvests and bereft of fertilizers, are impoverished and do not yield well. Erosion which ravages many valleys condemns the soil to slow but certain death. The great forests which once extended to the highest mountain peaks have, over the past two centuries, fallen victim to axe and fire. Each generation of peasants, more numerous than the last, carved out the arable land it needed and in the process destroyed such species as mahogany, oak and cottonwood. Deforestation thus exposes a thin and unstable soil to tropical downpours : in the rainy season, many tons of humus are swept into the sea by flooding rivers and the rushing torrents which carve the mountainsides into a thousand ravines. During a thunderstorm one day, a Marbial peasant, watching the Gosseline causing devastation along its banks and carrying away the good earth in its wild eddies, remarked with sadness and resignation : "There goes our life !"

What is more, Haiti is unfortunately situated in the path of the hurricanes. From time to time, as in 1952, one of them hits part of the island, laying low trees spared by man, carrying away houses as if they were made of straw; within a few hours the landscape is so transformed as to make it unrecognizable to somebody who has known it all his life.

When passing through the Haitian countryside it is easy to forget that, in those little huts hidden in the greenery, there live undernourished families haunted by the specter of drought or the payment of arrears. How can one remember misery, disease and children dying like flies, when one hears the laughter of washerwomen echoing along the limpid rivers, or think of erosion and its consequences when enjoying the freshness of a coffee grove or the deep shade of a giant cotton tree? If the denizen of the *mornes* is often miserable it is therefore not from a lack of " courage "—a term he so often uses and which, to him, means hard work and effort. Left to himself, illiterate, cut off from the outside world, how can he do better? He has made as much as possible of the meager African heritage which survived the days of enslavement. The immense upheavals of the modern world have awakened new aims and ambitions in him. He wants to change his life, to fight erosion, improve his land— and chiefly he wants to learn. Dimly he perceives that he must take his fate between his own hands and obtain by his own exertions what he so long expected as a gift from others.

The manner of cultivation practiced by the peasant is, by the way, not as rudimentary as sometimes alleged. It is often well enough adapted to the nature of the soil and the disposition of the property. Like his African ancestors, the peasant works the earth with a hoe, an implement which damages a thin layer of soil less than a plow, the use of which is in any case precluded by the contours of the land. To compensate in some measure for cramped holdings and troublesome broken up properties, maize, peas, sweet potatoes, manioc and yams are grown on the same plot : these, together with bananas, are the staple foods. Fruit trees and a kind of kitchen garden, or *diabdiab*, grown around the houses constitute a sort of reserve against rainy days and are, for that reason, jealously guarded.

Anybody who has lived in a Haitian valley will recall those African rhythms which, wafted across by the wind, suddenly break the morning silence. Many travelers imagine that these sounds accompany the performance of some mysterious rites, but the facts are more prosaic. Songs, the beating of drums and the blowing of conches are used merely to lighten the task of peasant co-operative work groups clearing some " square " of land, or pulling up the weeds threatening to choke young crops. Haitian writers have invested such manifestations of rural co-operation with poetic significance and elevated them to the rank of venerable African traditions which might be transformed into new ways of working the land. In point of fact, team work is a necessity from which the peasant cannot escape. In order to be able to satisfy his hunger, he must cultivate stretches too big for him and his family to manage alone. Furthermore, the short seasons force him to work quickly so that his fields may be ready for the life-giving rains. He therefore needs the help of others, as others need his help.

The *combite* (from the Spanish " convite "—invitation), or *corvée*, is the principal form of co-operative work. When a proprietor announces to his neighbors that he is organizing a big *combite* on such and such a day, all those summoned hurry along, no doubt moved partly by a spirit of solidarity, but also by the pleasure of meeting friends, singing and amusing oneself in a thousand ways, and by the eventual prospect of a copious meal. Not only has the " *combite* master " the satisfaction of seeing work done in a day which would otherwise have taken him weeks or obliged him to find improvised solutions, but he also has a means of raising his prestige and of gaining authority. If he does things on a generous scale, he will be known as a " Big Negro," a " Big Don," and will always be able to count on his neighbors' good will. It is no small matter to assemble a *combite* for a hundred or even fifty people. Providing food for all of them will not suffice. To prove the host's wealth and generosity something must be left over. A successful *combite* is one of which it can be said : " *Moun lignê a pèd dé vi. Mâjé rété a tè kô sa ! Nég té kòn fè, oui !...* " (" People were strung out as far as the eye could see. Food was spread on the ground like that. Here's a man who knows how things ought to be done, yes ! ")

The workers get into line and advance together, like soldiers. They are thrown into the attack on a field to be cleared or weeded by drums or a band of *vaccines* (bamboo trumpets) accompanying a kind of rustic bard, the *simidor*, or *samba*. It is his duty to intone the songs which the workers then repeat in chorus, marking the rhythms by bringing down their hoes. The *combite* songs are generally improvisations on themes drawn from local scandals, the ridiculous behavior of comrades or a political event. The *simidor* avoids actually naming those at whom he jeers, but the allusions escape nobody. That is why he is called " Judas." Some examples will illustrate the type of thing in question :

WORK SONGS

Yo fè espré, o, yo fè espré　　　They do it on purpose, oh, they do it on purpose,
Poum' sa mâdé charité, wo　　　So that I can apply for charity,
Ki paròl mwê tâdé o Bô Dié　　　Oh ! Good heavens, what's this I hear said ?

CHORUS

Yo fè espré, o, yo fè espré　　　They do it on purpose, oh, they do it on purpose,
Poum' sa mâdé charité, wo　　　So that I can apply for charity,
Ki paròl mwê tâdé o Bô Dié.　　　Oh ! Good heavens, what's this I hear said ?

La pli nâ mê Bô Dié lâné sa.
Pa di mâgo'm fini ané isit.

The rain this year is in God's hands.
Don't tell me my mangoes are no good this year!

Sé rôté
Daniel ki gê dé fâm
Pral môté lotel sêt Adré

It's a shame,
Daniel, who has two women already,
Is going to the altar (to marry) at Saint-André.

Pinga nou kôsilté
Daniel ki prâ you fâm.

Let's beware of taking advice from
Daniel who has taken spouse.

* * *

The conduct of operations is left to peasants who have a gift for leadership and a sense of responsibility. They are given the rank of " governor, " " director " or " squad commander. " They fix the quotas, haul shirkers over the coals, unmask malingerers and inspire the workers with voice and gestures. " Lift up your hands," they cry, " you're nearly through. The meal is cooking."

Despite the zeal of the leaders, a *combite's* task is performed rather incoherently by fits and starts. Some members stop to chat, others try out a dance step, and sometimes a worker in the mood for improvisation makes up a rhyming couplet inspired by some trivial incident. When a *combite* becomes sizable, the workers are split up into competing teams, each of which strives to be the first to finish its job on the particular " layer " (portion of a field) to which it has been assigned. One team can attempt to encircle another. The winners celebrate their victory in song or by a satirical couplet improvised by their *samba*.

Work is interrupted by snacks : fruit and small rations of grog are passed round to " keep up courage. " The band announces the resumption of the task with special beats. During this time, the women of the household are busy around big cauldrons in which slices of meat, corn semolina, peas, bananas and yams are being cooked. When the food is ready, the " director " comes along to taste it and to investigate its quality, or, more especially, the available quantity. If the meal is adjudged to be both tasty and copious the musicians beat out the signal for a general gathering. " Governors " and " directors " are responsible for dishing out, which is a delicate job, since everybody must be satisfied, while outstanding workers are specially rewarded. The meal is washed down with *clairin* (white rum) and often ends with dancing, which may go on all night.

The *combite* has brought into being curious institutions which may be found, in one form or another, throughout the entire Negro world. These are permanent mutual-aid societies. Peasants who cannot afford a *combite* get together into " work societies " whose members, in turn, may claim a *ronde* — that is to say, a whole or half a day of work on their own lands. The rules of such associations allow any participant to sell his claim to a day's work to some richer peasant. In this case, the acquired right covers not only the seller's own wage but also that of his fellows, all of which adds up to a considerable sum. Some work societies make a habit of selling their services, and the money thus earned is distributed to each of the members in turn. Furthermore, if one of their number falls ill, his comrades come to tend his gardens and to bring him medicines.

By emphasizing only the utilitarian aspect of these societies, however, one tends to misrepresent their essential nature. One of their aims—and not the least important—is to provide their members with amusement and to satisfy the love of ceremonial and acting which is so much alive among the peasants.

An element of play and even of pronounced farce enters into their most strictly economic activities. Each *corvée* gives rise to a kind of play on military or political themes. A work society is like an army or a miniature Republic of Haiti generously garnished, as in the " time of the bayonets " (civil wars), with officers and civil servants of the higher ranks. Often, the officers are more numerous than the " common people " or privates. In the

society known as the "Fleur de rose" ten out of fifteen members held some rank and the others complained of their humble status and aspired to the dignity of office. Besides a president and his ministers, each society includes generals and governors. Their duties are varied, but, of course, it is all make believe. Though the "governors" do actually lead the team on the job, the role of "*général-silence*" is confined to silencing those whose chatter is considered inopportune. Some resounding titles exist merely to tickle the imagination and the ear of their holders, and their origin often lies simply in a pun. The president of one society explained to me that the "finance minister" was the one who "finalized" everything and that the "county sheriff" was one who "counted" to see that all the work was done. Some ranks are also open to women who go under the title of "queen" followed by a descriptive label such as "bayonet," "flag," "basket," "director." Their functions elude precise definition even more than those of the men. The "queens" are much in evidence during festivals and dances, and are very active during the big *corvées* organized at coffee picking time.

Within the work societies, discipline and order are regulated according to precise rules. If a member fails to respond to the call without good excuse, the whole team descends on his home and "seizes" it for punishment. The society's flag is run up outside his door, and, if he refuses to explain his conduct, a goat from his herd is killed and the bananas are picked from his gardens so that the society may regale itself at his expense. The similarity between work societies and small states goes so far that a guilty individual, like a political refugee, has the right to seek asylum in a "consulate"—in practice, the home of an influential citizen. If the president of a society fails to fulfil his duties, the members come to "camp" on him : this is equivalent to mutinied soldiers coming to pillage.

Despite its old-fashioned character, the rural economy is not closed and is based on money. The peasant is thus obliged to come by money in order to clothe himself and to purchase all those various articles which he does not make himself. The chief source of cash is coffee and, in some regions, bananas, sisal or cotton. But coffee is the staple commodity on which the welfare of the peasant and the whole population depends. Every peasant strives to own coffee shrubs growing in the shade of protective trees planted near his house. So great is the love of the coffee shrubs that one peasant, having agreed to have his pruned by an agronomist, got such a shock when he saw the branches dropping that he fell down in a swoon.

As soon as the peasant has scratched a few savings together he buys, according to his means, a cow, a pig, a horse or simply some chickens, which he raises in the hope of selling them again for a profit if short of money. To him, domestic animals are the equivalent of a deposit in a savings bank : hence the term "interest" which he sometimes uses to describe them.

Intense commercial activity is carried on in the Haitian countryside, marked by the ceaseless coming and going of those heavily burdened women whom one meets any time after dawn on the roads and paths, for all the movement of goods and money is a feminine province. It is the women who are animated by the trading spirit, though there is something

pitiful about all this business which calls for a wealth of ingenuity and immense physical effort for ridiculous returns. Women will not hesitate to walk for two or three days in the sun, carrying loads of 80 lbs. on their heads, to be able to show a profit of three or four gourdes.[1] As soon as they hear that a certain product is being sold a few cents cheaper in a distant valley, they are off, climbing steep *mornes*, sleeping out under the stars and returning home mightily proud of the thin profit they have made, thanks to their initiative. They are in general quite unable to calculate their monthly or annual profits, though they know very well what they need to earn every day in order to " manage," and count neither their time nor their trouble.

Many peasant women who have collected a small sum by making sacrifices or borrowing at steep rates of interest spend it on the purchase of *kola* (a sweet, slightly fizzy drink), spices or hardware, in quantities just sufficient to stock a small stall. They set up " shop " in a shed or under a mango tree at a crossing of paths or simply along the wayside. Those who specialize in the sale of *kola*, white rum and sweets lead a vagabond's life. No get-together—be it for a voodoo ceremony, a cockfight, a political assembly, a wedding or a death-watch—escapes them. They are the first to hear of it by *télédyol* (bush telegraph) and the first to arrive. For nights on end their little kerosene lamps are lit around the houses where people celebrate. They sit quite still, utterly indifferent to the joys or sorrows of others, worried only about the coppers collecting in their belts.

Once a week, the market brings this mercantile fever to a head. Starting early in the morning, an uninterrupted procession of women approaches along the paths leading to it ; some push a heavily laden donkey in front of them or sit astride the beast's pack-saddle, their legs dangling. Most of them, however, come on foot. Their waists girt with a kerchief " to give them strength," they progress rapidly, carrying enormous baskets or a *bac* (tray) on their heads. In this

[1] The gourde is worth $0.20.

endless file, men are in a minority. They go to market only to sell their cattle or some home made articles, or simply as idlers, to drink a round of grog with friends, discuss the prices or the cockfights, or to hear the latest news from the valley. Many young men come along merely in the hope of picking up girls.

Having arrived at the market, the women take up their usual pitches in a shed or in the sun. They spread out their wares, and those who have not brought a chair along squat on their heels, decently drawing their skirts down between their legs. Without pestering them with sales talk, they patiently await customers behind their stalls. At most, they will encourage those who seem to be taking a certain interest in their wares, and assure them that they give " honest " measure. Sometimes, a marketwoman who wishes to sell out her stock will cry: " *Pillage, pillage!* " thus indicating that she is willing to unload everything at cut rates.

Buying is always associated with much haggling. In such exchanges, the miming of the participants is every bit as expressive as their words. The market-woman pretends to be outraged by the reductions suggested to her: she withdraws or covers up her wares as if to hide them from the sight of frivolous folk, not worthy of being allowed to look at them. Further, she affects a sulky air and turns her head away, only to burst suddenly into violent abuse in simulated anger. She calls upon the entire market to witness the wrong being done to her.

The customers, on the other hand, examine the goods with deliberation and distaste. Sometimes, having handled and felt the weight of each individual fruit from a small pile worth one tenth of a gourde, they pretend to be going, with sharp cries of protest. At this moment the marketwoman changes her tactics and gives in, or persuades them, in conciliatory tones, to pay the price she is asking. A little scene which I witnessed in Marbial can perhaps convey some idea of the lack of proportion between the output of energy and the stakes involved in a transaction. Attracted to a group by loud voices, I listened for an hour to a

discussion between a local "stallholder" and an itinerant seller who was offering the former maize semolina. Agreement on the price had been reached, but the buyer wished to use her own bowl as a measure : it happened to be very slightly larger than that of the seller. This tiny difference was to yield her profit.

Payment also gives rise to diverting comedies. The customer, as if stricken with paralysis, is unable to find her money. She hesitates for some time and then, despite herself, hands over her coins one by one. She stops from time to time, hoping that the seller will declare herself to be satisfied and that she can thus begin to haggle anew. But the other woman insists dryly on her dues and threatens to take back her wares. When the agreed sum has at last been paid, it must be counted again and again, for, as the saying goes, money is made " to be counted. " It may happen that an unscrupulous customer tries to muddle the market-woman by assuring her that she has already paid part of the price. Cries and curses then fly about, and there are mutual threats to call in " the State " (the police). For certain wares, the buyer insists on a *dégi* — or " bonus. " In other words, she requires a small supplement in the shape of a slightly overfilled measure instead of one filled to the brim ; the little extra cone is called a *tignon* (head-scarf).

The promiscuity of the work gangs split up the African family. Only rarely did the masters favor marriage between slaves. On the contrary, they encouraged concubinage in order " to be able to separate without difficulty the members of one family, or rather the inhabitants of one hut, which was a real way of spreading debauchery among the Negroes and causing the sterility which is perhaps the most terrible accusation to be laid against slavery " (Vassière). During the period of isolation and stagnation when the Haitian peasantry as we know it today began to emerge, the rural family assumed a pattern not ideally adapted to a nation whose laws and official standards are modeled on the Christian West.

The peasant is much blamed for practicing polygamy. It is tolerated, although, as we have seen, less widespread than often alleged. Above all, it is the privilege of rich " dons " who own dispersed estates and have the means to set up several homes which they visit in turn. One would be hard put to say whether this practice is due to the survival of African customs, to a demographic situation characterized by a slight excess of women, or simply to economic motives. Peasant polygamy differs in many ways from its counterpart in Africa where the husband is surrounded by his wives, who live either under the same roof with him or each in a separate hut. A man can rarely make his wife or mistress accept the presence of a rival in Haiti : although custom permits polygamy, the women obey a different moral code and cannot bridle their jealousy. When a wife or mistress meets the woman who is sharing the favors of her " husband," her *matelote* (shipmate), as they say in Haiti, then a swearing match, peppered with insults and threats, breaks out. It is on such occasions that there are the " scandals " which call for the intervention of the rural constable and end up before the justice of the peace.

Plaçage, or common law marriage, is the most widespread form of conjugal union in rural Haiti. Townspeople refer to it disdainfully as concubinage, which is most mis-

leading because *plaçage* is accepted and sanctioned by custom and public opinion. It certainly lacks the respectability of legal marriages, but if it has been contracted according to the established rules and if the couple " live decently " with each other, the difference is very slight. Nor is it for moral reasons that the peasant proposes to enter into marriage with all its appropriate trappings. A wedding celebrated with every traditional pomp raises the prestige of the families which pay for it, demonstrates how well off they are, determines their rank in the social scale and gives proof of their *savoir-vivre*. Hence the idea of an inexpensive wedding never even occurs to the majority of peasants. If they cannot afford what is considered to be the price of a proper wedding, they would rather do without. Shortage of money is the usual reason advanced by peasants when asked why they have not married the woman with whom they are living and who is the mother of their numerous progeny. Many priests denounce this taste for ostentation from their pulpits in an effort to deprive their parishioners of a pretext for getting out of marriage. They exhort young couples to marry in the simplest of clothes, even, if necessary, barefoot, but the faithful think this is merely a joke in poor taste, or even a sign of contempt. To please the priest, some marry in church in the clothes recommended, but after the ceremony they hurry out to don the veils, dresses and traditional suits before joining their families and guests. Without doubt the desire to do things properly is not the only reason behind the reluctance of many peasants to legalize their unions. Many are scared stiff of binding themselves with documentary evidence and consider that, not knowing what life may hold in store for them, it is better to stick to custom and not to create unnecessary difficulties. It cannot be denied, moreover, that conjugal unions, whether legal or common law, are today unstable and that couples who remain faithful to each other over many years are in a minority. But this is perhaps a phenomenon caused by the disorder of rural society in an era of crisis. Nevertheless, it would be misleading to equate *plaçage* with libertinage. In her own home, a *placée* has all the duties of a wife (especially that of being faithful), and also all her rights as mistress of the house.

Marriage and *plaçage* are preceded by a number of steps laid down in the hallowed rules forming part of a fastidious etiquette inherited by the peasants from their dual background of African and French traditions. The proposal of marriage (or *plaçage*) is made by the parents of the young man, who visit those of the girl to hand them a " letter of application." The latter has been composed by a public scribe in French, the noble language which alone is fit to be used in so important a matter. It must be handwritten on special paper decorated with flowers and with an open-work border. Here is the text of one of these letters (with an approximate transliteration into English) :

" Aux Messieurs et dames Adoctéris Das Phizelia petit mouché et Precis Millord —
Messieurs et dames Je prend ma plume en vous écrivant cette lettre de demande pour vous demandé la main de votre fille roselie que Je désire avoir pour épouse. Je souhaite de trouvis en vous une satisfaction très agréable et admirable.
recevez Messieurs et dames mes salutations très distingué."

5 March 1936

" To

Sirs and madams Adoctéris Das
Phizelia petit mouché and Precis Millord—

Sirs and madams I take my pen in writing you this
letter of request to ask the hand of your daughter
roselie who I wish to have as spouse. I hope to obtain
your very agreeable and admirable satisfaction.

Sirs and madams my best greetings."

The letter is placed in a mahogany casket wrapped
in a silken cloth. Sometimes a few gourdes are slipped
in as well, to reward the scholar who is going to read it out. The parcel is delivered by a
member of the family selected for his age or importance. The girl's parents welcome the
visitors courteously and offer them refreshments, but they are careful not to mention the
object of the call. This indifference is merely assumed, because all of them have reached an
agreement beforehand. The refusal of an offer made with such solemnity would be regarded
as a deadly insult and would start a permanent feud between the two families. Some days later

it is the turn of the girl's parents to deliver the " letter of reply ," also wrapped in silk.

When the union has received the blessing of both families, the young man constructs the hut, which he will share with his future companion, on land given him by his father. When the poles of a hut can be seen on the peak of a *morne*, the peasants say : " Well, well, so-and-so is going to take a wife. . . ." The family does not only consist of those flesh and blood persons who are related to each other, but also of the dead and the guardian spirits, who must be informed of the planned alliance during the course of a " service." Some spirits, fearing that the future wife or husband may neglect them, express their disagreement and demand gifts. It is thought best to placate them : a couple which does not enjoy the protection of the family spirits will never find bliss.

With its procession, its speeches and its banquets, the actual wedding ceremony might well be that of peasants in the Valais or in Normandy. The bride is most anxious to wear a

white veil, even if she is a mother. If one can manage to turn up at church on horseback, the wedding will be considered to be that much more elegant.

Anyone who is led to believe, by what has just been said about polygamy and common-law marriages, that peasant women live in a state of fear and submission, will be greatly struck by the ease of their bearing, the frankness of their speech and their resolute air. Judging by the prominence of women in economic activities and by their sense of responsibility, one might, with a certain amount of exaggeration, speak of a " matriarchy." By law and custom, man is certainly the master, and women do not challenge his authority. They are, in fact, eager to underline this in their conversation and in the deference shown to the " lord and master." But such submissiveness is formal rather than real : the women have control of the house and of the children ; they readily take part in their husband's business affairs and know how to stand up to him if necessary. Women owe this power to a division of

labor which had its origin in Guinea and which today still leaves them in command of the purse strings.

From the age of eight or nine, little girls are trained in commercial matters and expected to relieve their mothers behind the shop counter. There they learn to haggle with all the liveliness and patience of their elders, and to defend their interests with comical energy. It is a school which fast teaches them to fend for themselves and fight for their independence. Countless families depend upon the commercial acumen of the woman in order to make both ends meet. More than one middle class Haitian owes his rise in society to some peasant woman who has toiled ceaselessly and worked miracles of ingenuity to pay for his studies.

Haitian peasants love children and take pride in having many of them. It is not without a certain air of complacency that a man, when he is asked to do so, counts up the "little 'uns" he has fathered with his *placées* and at the same time promiscuously during passing *zafé* (affairs), though one would suppose that, under such conditions, the birth of a child would

merely be an additional burden. It must not be forgotten, however, that a child may cost money during the first few years of its life but that it quickly takes its share of domestic duties, and that at ten years of age it will mind cattle, climb trees to pick fruit, and begin to make use of agricultural implements. And do not numerous progeny mean that the parents will be cared for in old age, and enjoy the certainty of being given a " beautiful funeral " ?

Women, for their part, are proud of procreating : no infirmity is harder to bear than sterility. The birth of a child gives a woman a better claim to permanent support and, if she is a *placée*, holds out the hope of a gift of land or an inheritance. Few men refuse to recognize paternity and, unless they choose to behave like " vagabonds," they fulfill their obligations to the best of their abilities. At Marbial, the parents of a seduced girl never make a big issue out of the matter. Their pride suffers if, contrary to custom, they must take the first steps towards common law or legal marriage, but if no agreement can be reached the child is incorporated into the girl's family without difficulty. Children of previous liaisons are no bar to *plaçage*, and it is understood that a woman takes them along to her new home. During my researches in Marbial, I was surprised by the number of children of different parentage living in a single household. I have heard of wives who bring up their husband's children by other women and even declare themselves to be the legal mother so that the children might bear their father's name and inherit property from him.

Respect and obedience are the two habits parents try to drum into their children at an early age. Retribution awaits the disobedient child who becomes rebellious or kicks up a shindy. He may be sure to get a taste of the cane. When parents chastise, they don't do it gently. Piercing screams from the victim are intended to arouse the neighborhood and cause the intercession of some charitable soul who will cry: " Mercy, mercy." Even at twenty, a boy or girl will not escape a thrashing if he has been seriously at fault or failed to show respect to his parents. Though they have been called boorish, the peasants will punish severely any word or action which might be considered impolite. Children are taught not to interrupt the conversation of grownups, not to walk in front of them when they are sitting down, to look at the ground when spoken to and not to *coupé jé* (bat their eyelids as a sign of the sulks or anger). Life itself teaches them the fear of wrongdoing, theft being only one degree lower than murder in the scale of crime. Children don't easily forget the spectacle of the guilty, ignominiously tied with rope and carrying the *corpus delicti*—most commonly an animal—all the way to the town prison under the escort of the local *maréchal*.

Peasant education tends to develop responsibility in children. At no more than five or six years of age, they are given a chicken, a goat, a pig or even a cow by their parents or godparents to look after. Any money made through the sale of these beasts or their young is spent on buying clothes or other animals. A little boy who has no goats or pigs of his own takes some on *gadinaj*—that is to say, he raises them for their owner, half the proceeds going to the owner and the other half to the youngster. It is the special duty of one of the older children to look after the babies until they are four or five years old and can eat, walk, or dress themselves. At six years of age a child will be asked to mind the house when the grownups are out.

It is every peasant's ambition to send his children to school, and he will make any sacrifice in order to be able to do so. In remote regions without a local state school, they will club together to pay a teacher. To get to school, pupils must often walk for hours, climb *mornes* and cross torrents. In the hope of being able to read and write one day, they do not mind mumbling texts all day long which they don't understand because they are in French and taken from obsolete schoolbooks. He who manages to acquire the secret of reading and writing derives great prestige from it. He may become a public scribe, and will be called upon to decipher that incredible anthology of religious poetry called the *Marseilles* [1] during the death-watches.

Children's games are not very complicated: girls play with skipping ropes while boys make tops out of small oranges, set traps for buntings and wood-pigeons and try to catch eels in the river. Those who like music try to blow the bamboo trumpets, like their elders. At Marbial, there were two children's bands which featured little dancers, the youngest of whom were not yet three years old. By the age of twelve or thirteen, budding musicians can join a " bamboo trumpet club " or a *combite* band, with the rank of " major." In the evenings, children listen to their elders spinning yarns or asking riddles. This is their introduction to the wealth of African folklore, passed on by word of mouth, and further enriched by stories and themes drawn from the folklore of France.

---

[1] A collection of paraphrases of the Scriptures, mysteries, and lives of the saints, said to have originated in Marseilles.

Though the Haitian peasant calls himself a Catholic and thinks of himself as such, he has not, for all that, abandoned the gods of his ancestors. He continues to call upon them for spiritual comfort, protection from misfortune and cures for his ills. His worship of them is generally described under the name of "voodoo," a word of Dahomeyan origin meaning "spirit" or "god." This popular religion, which mixes pagan rites and beliefs with Catholic practices, has long stood in ill repute. An ambiguous and sinister legend has spread about the powers of its priests and the nature of its ceremonies, all of which has been carefully nurtured by many sensation-loving authors. For many people, and even for many upper-class Haitians, the word "voodoo" still conjures up scenes of mystical abandon, blood, obscenity; it is charged with the terror associated with every secret sect. Upper-class Haitians are rightly distressed by the very dubious reputation thus given to their country, but in reacting against the myth they show a tendency to belittle the importance of voodoo : they wish to prove that it is only a harmless bit of rural folklore with a touch of African background. Consolation should be found in the fact that Haiti is far from possessing a monopoly of Pagan-Christian cults. In Brazil and in Cuba, where voodoo flourishes under the names of "candomblé," "macumba," "chango," "santeria" or "ñaniguismo," it has its thousands —if not its millions—of adherents. Its public and secret rites are celebrated in more purely African style there, and with a brilliance which the modest "paganism" of the rural Haitian masses cannot hope to rival. Types of voodoo also flourish in Trinidad and Jamaica and even in New Orleans, where black and white magic is still called "hoodoo."

"One must be a Catholic to serve the *loa*...." This phrase, from the mouth of a peasant, excellently defines the attitude of the voodoo sectarians towards the Church. The peasant bringing sacrifices to the family guardian spirits, attending ceremonies in the *houmfò* (temple) and responding to the call of the drums, does not think—or at least did not think, until quite recently—that he was mixing one religion with another. He would be greatly distressed if he could not have his children baptized, take Communion or call the priest to his bedside when he is dying. He attaches much importance to the sacraments, indeed too great an importance, according to the Church, for he believes them to have magical properties ! He looks upon the Christian duties as "obligations" which only a "tramp" would fail to observe. But the peasant is very ignorant of doctrine or religious history, and it must be admitted that for him, Catholicism wears the somewhat austere aspect of the cement chapels on top of the hills. It is voodoo which supplies the feeling of confidence mixed with fear and hope which lends human warmth to intercourse with the supernatural. Having coexisted for two centuries, Catholicism and African cults are finally merged into conception of a universe in which *le bon Dieu*, Jesus Christ, the Blessed Virgin, the saints and the spirits rub shoulders quite freely.

Until the clergy decided to stop such promiscuity, the voodoo worshippers were in no way troubled by their dual allegiance. They saw no harm in dancing all night in honor of the African gods, and then going to Mass, and it takes the mentality of a white to see anything offensive in a procession headed by a voodoo priest walking shamelessly at the side of the reverend father. Voodoo ritual has also borrowed heavily from Catholic liturgy. Usually, most services to African gods are introduced by Thanksgivings *(actions de grâces)* in front of an altar erected under a lace canopy and covered in pictures and candles; the priest *(houngan)* and priestess *(mambo)*, surrounded by their acolytes, recite *Paters, Aves, Confiteors,* followed by hymns to the Virgin and the saints. By thus giving a Catholic flavor to ceremonies which themselves are hardly Catholic, the voodoo worshippers hope to increase the effectiveness of their practices and to please the African gods. Prayers which they learned from the curés and which they hear recited in church possess a prestige and intrinsic value in their eyes, from which they would like their own religion to benefit.

Voodoo deities are known as *loa*, or " mysteries "; in some regions they are called " saints " or " angels." They are an odd crowd, almost impossible to count, since, apart from the " great *loa* " whom everybody has always known and respected, there exist many whose fame is recent and local, and who are worshipped by only a small group of initiates, or even by members of but one family. Though fresh recruits still come to swell the ranks of the *loa*, these are also thinned out by the oblivion into which many of the spirits fall when they no longer command any worshippers.

At the apex of the invisible world stands the " Good Lord," sometimes called the " Great Master," creator of the Universe, and believed to be a potentate holding sway over the *loa* and the saints. His name is constantly on the peasants' lips, but they do not fear him or even worry much about him. Like the supreme beings of many African religions, he plays the part of a distant and idle godhead, recognized somewhat hazily as an impersonal force, before whom all other beings—including other gods and spirits—must yield. To the voodoo devotee, the idea of God corresponds to what, in everyday speech, we mean by " fate " or " nature." Common ills, too widespread to be blamed on malicious spirits or on acts of witchcraft, and which we would simply call natural, are known in Haiti as " diseases of the Lord." Every time a peasant makes some plan, he is careful to say: " *Si Dyé vlé* " (God willing), less no doubt in order to subject himself to the will of God than in the hope of keeping bad luck at bay. The fact that a Haitian peasant exclaims: " Good Lord, good " after a misfortune has often been interpreted as a sign of his unshakable optimism. It is no more than an expression of resignation to a fate beyond his understanding.

The *loa* are subordinate to God and, like the faithful, are members of the Catholic church, since they are baptized and sometimes even ask for Communion; but though voodoo devotees call the spirits " saints," they do not confuse the two, and know they are of different origins. Catholic influence has persuaded voodoo worshippers of the necessity of placing pictures of African deities in their temples. They have found it convenient to use cheap color prints depicting Catholic saints for this purpose. The reasons for selecting the picture of a given saint to represent a certain *loa* are often disconcerting: it is some superficial and accidental detail which generally determines the choice. Damballah, the snake-god, has been identified with Saint Patrick only because the saint is shown on religious prints in the act of ridding Ireland of snakes. Saint James the Greater, who appears in Christian iconography in the guise of a knight in armor, has become Ogou-ferraille, god of iron and of war. It is therefore quite understandable that priests, during the anti-voodoo drives, have burned all holy pictures found in temples without the slightest hesitation while at the same time exhorting their flock to worship exactly the same images in churches and chapels. They realized that the voodoo worshippers had pressed these pictures into the service of their own gods and thereby deprived them of their specifically Christian significance.

No particular part of the universe is set aside as the abode of the gods and spirits. The *loa* are said to come from " Guinea," which, however, does not describe any exact geographical location. It is simply a vague place which the gods and spirits leave when they are summoned to earth. Gods and spirits also haunt mountains, rocks, caves, springs and ponds ; many live on the beds of rivers or in the depths of the sea. The *houngans* and *mambos* go to visit them and return vested with fresh powers. " Mysteries " are also present in the sacred trees *(arbres-reposoirs)* which grow around temples and houses in the country. The giant *Ceiba* trees sometimes grow to colossal size : this and the impression of power which they convey have caused them to survive as objects of worship in spite of all attempts to discourage the practice. Peasants bring sacrifices to them, hang lengths of woven materials from their branches and burn candles at their roots.

Loa differ from ordinary mortals only in the breadth of their " knowledge," or supernatural powers, which comes to the same thing. They are all men of the soil sharing the tastes, habits and passions of their worshippers. Like them, they are fond of good living, wily, touchy, ribald, jealous and subject to short but violent fits of rage. They have their preferences among one another and choose to associate or keep apart just like the most humble " denizens " of the countryside. As we shall see, their behavior when they make terrestrial appearances is often not at all what might be expected of supernatural beings. Gods though they are, they may be rude, swear, drink to excess, beg, pick quarrels with other *loa* or play schoolboy tricks on each other.

Only a few of the Haitian gods can be introduced here, and these have been chosen from among the most powerful and popular. In so brief a list, Legba must take first place. He still occupies a privileged position in the religion of Dahomey and Nigeria because he is the interpreter of the gods. Only he can translate men's prayers and transmit them to the invisible powers. In Africa, his symbol, which is to be seen outside every hut and at the entrance to villages, is a heap of earth surmounted by a phallus. In Haiti, Legba has undergone some changes of character. Far from being a phallic deity, he has become a limping old man, leaning on crutches and hobbling along. He is nevertheless a god since he is the master of the mystical barrier which divides the divine from the profane world. Legba must open the barrier to allow the faithful to invoke the other *loa* :

Atibô Legba, l'ouvri bayè pou mwê	Atibo Legba, open the barrier for me,
Papa Legba, l'ouvri bayè pou mwê	Papa Legba, open the barrier for me,
Pou mwê pasé	To let me through,
Lò m'a tounê, m'a salié loa-yo	When I come back I will salute the *loa*
Vodou Legba, l'ouvri bayè pou mwê	Voodoo Legba, open the barrier for me,
Lo m'a tounê, m'a remésyé loa-yo Abobo.	When I return, I will thank the *loa*.

Guardian of the earthly gates and walls, he also watches over homes, roads and paths. Under the name of " Maître Carrefour " (Master of the Crossroads) he receives the homage of sorcerers who go to crossroads to practice the mysteries of their profession.

The sea, its fauna and flora, as well as the ships which sail it and those who live from its bounty, are under the jurisdiction of Agwé-taroyo. He is invoked under the names of " Sea shell," " Eel " or " Pond tadpole." His emblems are miniature boats, blue or green paddles, shells, madrepores and sometimes also small metal fish. The voodoo Neptune is represented as a mulatto with fair skin and green eyes. He loves the sound of cannon. Many people imagine that the salvoes fired when warships enter the roads off Port-au-Prince are in his honor. He is naturally the protector of seafarers, and it is to him that they turn in the hour of danger :

Mèt Agoué, kòté ou yé	Master Agwé, where are you ?
Ou pa oué mwê nâ résif	Can't you see I'm on the reef ?
Agoué-taroyo, kòté ou yé	Agwé-taroyo, where are you ?
Ou pa oué mwê sou lâ mè	Can't you see I'm on the sea ?
M'gê zavirô nâ mê mwê	I have an oar in my hand,
m'pa sa tounê déyè	I cannot turn back,
M'douvâ déja	I am going forward,
Mèt Agoué, woyo kòté ou yié mwê	Master Agwé, where am I ?
Ou pa oué mwê nâ résif	Can't you see I'm on the reef ?

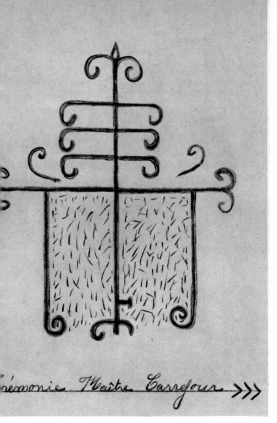

Cérémonie Maître Carrefour ⟫⟫

Agoüta Royo

Agwé's festivals take place along the shore where the symbolic boat is carried in procession. His favorite dishes and the drinks he prefers (notably champagne) are placed on a *bac*—a rack made of superimposed boxes, painted blue and decorated with marine designs. The god's worshippers, dressed in white, hire a sailing craft and set off for Les Islets, a famous reef off Port-au-Prince. The ship is decked out with streamers, flags flutter in the breeze, drums beat, and the faithful dance, after a fashion, on deck or in the hold. When the craft arrives alongside the reefs, one or more white sheep are thrown overboard, followed by the *bac* and a few fowls which have been attached to it. After the sacrifice, one must withdraw as quickly as possible without looking back, in order not to offend the god who, like the kings of Dahomey, does not like to be watched while eating.

Fields and agricultural work are the province of Zaka, the " minister of agriculture " in the world of the gods. The peasant god par excellence, he is to be approached like any country neighbor and familiarly called " cousin." He is always dressed peasant-fashion : a straw hat, a rough blue smock, a *macoute* (straw satchel) slung over his shoulder, and a short clay pipe in his mouth. Even in character, Zaka is a real peasant of the *mornes* : he is suspicious, avid for gain, likes wrangling and detests city folk.

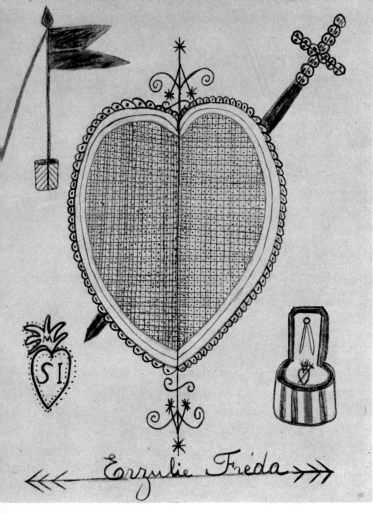

In Dahomey, Gu is the blacksmith of the gods. Since the working of iron has lost much of its importance in Haiti he has become solely a warrior god and is represented by a sword stuck in the ground. His features and manners are often modeled on those of old veterans of the time of the civil wars.

Ezili-Freda-Dahomey has often been compared to Aphrodite. The two goddesses resemble each other to the extent to which a pretty West Indian mulatto can be compared with a Homeric deity. Like the Greek goddess, Ezili belongs to a group of sea gods, but she has quite abandoned her original element and become almost exclusively the personification of beauty and feminine charm. She also has all the faults of a spoiled and pretty woman, being flirtatious, sensual, avid for luxury and pleasure, and an unbridled spendthrift. In every temple, one room is reserved for Ezili. Her pink and white dresses and her jewels are kept there; on a dressing table, a wash basin, towel, soap, comb, lipstick, nailbrush and orange-stick are laid out for her.

One of the most famous of the voodoo deities is Damballah-wèdo, the snake god, who long gave rise to the idea that the Haitian peasants were ophiolaters. As a snake god, Damballah particularly haunts springs, lakes and ponds, of which he is guardian. Like his wife, Aida-wèdo, he is compared to the rainbow, which, in voodoo cosmogony, is nothing more than a heavenly serpent.

Certain kinds of gods readily respond to the solicitations of sorcerers and are quite willing to become the instruments of secret vengeance. Marinette-bwa-chèch (Marinette of the dry arm), Petit-Jean-pieds-fins (Johnny of the delicate feet) and Ezili-jé-rouge (Red-eyed Ezili) are the most famous of these vindictive *loa*. The other

Dam - ·XX· Balah

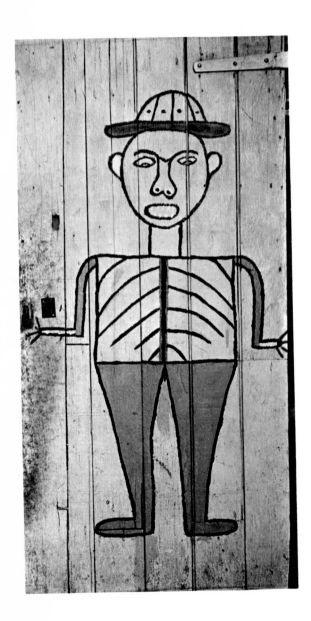

agents of magic are the dead, but they can only serve the sorcerers if Baron-Samedi, Baron-Cimetière or Baron-la-Croix are prepared to release them.

Sorcery and necromancy are within the power of Baron-Samedi and of the spirits of the Guédé family which he heads. In the last resort, the efficacy of evil spells and magic poisons depends on him, for if Baron and the gods around him refuse to cause the victim selected for them to perish, no rites or invocations have any effect. Even the most powerful gods cannot execute sentence of death unless Baron and the Guédé agree to help them. The rural conception of Baron is derived from the employees of undertakers to be seen at stylish funerals: top hat, black suit, white gloves, starched cuffs and a black cane. These accessories are sometimes hung in voodoo temples from the big black crosses which symbolize Baron. His other emblem—skull and crossbones —is painted on the altars or the big calabashes in which he is offered his food. Gravediggers' implements—spade, pick and hoe—are also numbered among his emblems, and he is sometimes represented by these objects in triplicate and called " Trois-pelles," " Trois-piquois," " Trois-houes."

Baron-Samedi's wife, Brigitte, or Madame Brigitte, also exercises authority over cemeteries, especially those where the first person buried happens to have been a woman. Many gods belonging to the Guédé family were born as a result of a union between the goddess and Baron, such as General Jean-Baptiste-Tracé (General John Baptist the Outliner) who " outlines " the boundaries of graves; General Fouillé (General Dig) who "digs" the graves, Guédémasaka, Guédé-vi, Guédé-ti-wavé, Avant-Garde-Brutus and many others with similarly evocative names. All these supernatural beings are more or less closely connected with death and its attendant rites. As we shall discover when we come to discuss possession provoked by the Guédé, these funeral deities are facetious and fall easily into obscenity.

" The *loa* love us, protect and watch over us. They show us what is happening to our relatives living far away and they tell us what medicines will do us good when we are sick. If we are hungry, they appear to us in dreams and say : ' Don't despair, you will soon earn some money,' and the money comes."

This declaration of belief made by a peasant woman summed up for me what voodoo devotees expect from their gods. She might, however, have added : " The *loa* inform us of the plots being hatched by our enemies . . ."

Cures for many a reputedly incurable disease are often ascribed to the *loa*, who advise either the priest giving treatment or the patient himself, to whom they appear in dreams. They also succor the destitute and help them find jobs. But the *loa's* protection is never entirely gratuitous. Those who benefit therefrom incur definite " obligations " towards them, the most important of which are, of course, the sacrifices and offerings which must be brought at more or less regular intervals.

In Haiti, gods, like men, are extremely touchy and any trifle can give offence. The gods are particularly sensitive in matters of ritual. Simply forgetting to dance the number of *rondes* to which they believe themselves entitled, or serving them dishes they dislike, incurs their immediate ire and makes them ready to pounce. They may even resent imprudent words uttered by their worshippers in a temper, and it is not unusual for the *loa* to visit upon children the sins of their parents.

It is said of a person exposed to the vengeance of a *loa* that " the god has gripped him." Most frequently, the *loa* afflict the guilty with a disease the gravity of which is sometimes out of all proportion to the offence, for the *loa* are hotheaded rather than just. Madness, too, is nearly always held to be a supernatural punishment. The shadowy and arbitrary character ascribed to the *loa* accounts for the acceptance of punishments without much protest, and those persecuted by them usually appeal to their sense of mercy rather than to their sense of justice. They are summoned by *mangers* (feasting)—that is to say, by sacrifices of animals and offerings of food made to them during the ceremonies held in their honor. The need to serve the *loa* is so urgent that peasants working in towns will return

to their homes when they believe the time to have come to feed their *loa*, or else make some arrangement with a priest so that he can fulfill their duties for them.

Voodoo worshippers are divided into cult groups centered around a temple, or *houmfò*. This belongs to a priest *(houngan)* or priestess who directs the ceremonies and serves as intermediary between the believers and the supernatural powers. The priests are attended by *hounsi*, or " servants of the gods," who assist them in their offices and make up both the corps de ballet and the choir of the temple. *Hounsi* are chosen from among the *kanzo*, those who have been fully initiated. Very little is known about the long and costly preliminary ceremonies since initiates must keep them strictly secret.

There is hardly any difference between the " houses of the mysteries " and those of ordinary folk. A Haitian *houmfò* is not a temple in the usual sense of the term but a religious center that can be likened to the dwelling place of a large family. There are *houmfò* consisting only of one shack and others which resemble a hamlet. Often they are merely covered areas and a main structure which shelters both the gods and the family of the priest or priestess.

The only characteristic by which *houmfò* may be identified from outside is their peristyle, a sort of open shelter offering protection from inclement weather to voodoo dances and ceremonies. The roof is held up by gaudy posts : the one in the center, the *poteau-mitan*, acts as the pivot of ritual dances and is venerated during the ceremonies as evidence of its particular holiness. It is the " way of the spirits," the ladder by which the spirits climb down into the peristyle when summoned.

The sanctuary, or *bagi*, is a room at the far end of which there are more altars. These are brick platforms of about table height with one or several arched recesses in front. The *bagi* is a veritable junk shop of ritualistic objects : jugs containing either *loa* or souls, bowls of the Sacred Twins, pots containing the souls of the initiated, thunderstones or *loa* stones in oil, playing cards, rattles and divine emblems of every description. Holy pictures are pinned to the walls and Ogu's sword is stuck in the ground in front of the altar.

The ceremonies are conducted by the *houngan* (priest) or the *mambo* (priestess), who hold a rattle in their hands as a symbol of office. They are assisted by a *la-place*, a kind of master of ceremonies, and a *houngenikon* who conducts the choirs and directs the dances. The peasants' love of parades and their highly developed hierarchical consciousness is reflected in many aspects of the cult. A special drum tattoo having summoned the worshippers, the " servants of the gods," clad in white, march out of the temple ; they are preceded by gold-spangled flags and by the *la-place* twirling his saber with all the dash of a cavalry officer. One after another they come to kiss the earth first in front of the *poteau-mitan*, then in front of the drums of the band and lastly in front of the " master of the *houmfò*," who graciously helps them up and makes them do three pirouettes. All greet each other as equals and " twirl " one another. These mutual courtesies, which recur throughout the ceremonies, express all the fine shades of respect or condescension laid down by the strongly hierarchical character of the cult groups. Even the gods are not exempt from such exercises in politeness.

Dancing is intimately linked with worship and indeed takes so prominent a place in it that voodoo might almost be defined as a " dance religion." The drums beating out dance rhythms have to some extent become the very symbols of voodoo, so much so that " beating the drum " conveys, in current speech, the idea of " celebrating the *loa* rites." Though the drummer may be no more than a professional musician who, often enough, has never been initiated, he is nevertheless the life and soul of every ceremony. He must combine a very keen sense of rhythm and a remarkable musical memory with an uncommon degree of nervous resistance. Drummers play their instruments all through the night with a fierce passion which is occasionally quite frenzied. One might infer, from their screwed up eyes, their contorted faces and the rattle in their throats, that they had fallen under the spell of some spirit, were it not rare for a musician to be actually possessed. For voodoo worshippers, a drum is more than a sacred instrument : it is the vessel of a deity. Drums are worshipped, and marks of respect are showered upon them.

The very varied drumbeats, named after the African tribes which introduced them to Haiti, govern the steps and movements of the dancers. They also invoke numerous families of gods since dancing is a ritualistic act releasing mystic forces which work on the " invisibles." Music and dancing please the gods because they, too, are dancers carried away by the magic of rhythm. The faithful revolve about the *poteau-mitan* in no particular order, each one making up his own steps except in the rather common cases when two or more dancers face each other and compete in agility and invention. The art of dancing is expressed less through the movement of the feet than through that of the shoulders and hips. A favorite movement for women is to grip the hem of their dresses with both hands, raising and lowering it in time to the music ; the men let their slightly crooked arms dangle, as if to keep their balance. In the *yanvalou*, one of the most popular dances, the body is bent forward, the knees are allowed to sag and the shoulders are perpetually, restlessly undulating—a continuous movement which seems to emanate literally from the spine.

Songs are used as accompaniments to all dances, and even to the chief parts of the ritual. They are short pieces of music—sometimes of European origin—sung in the African manner,

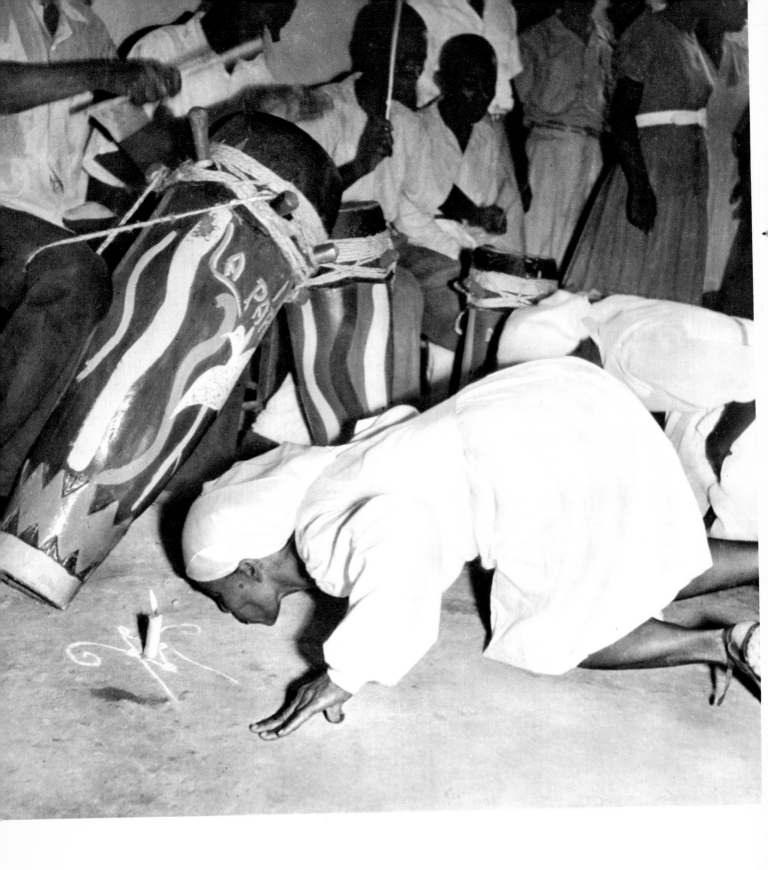

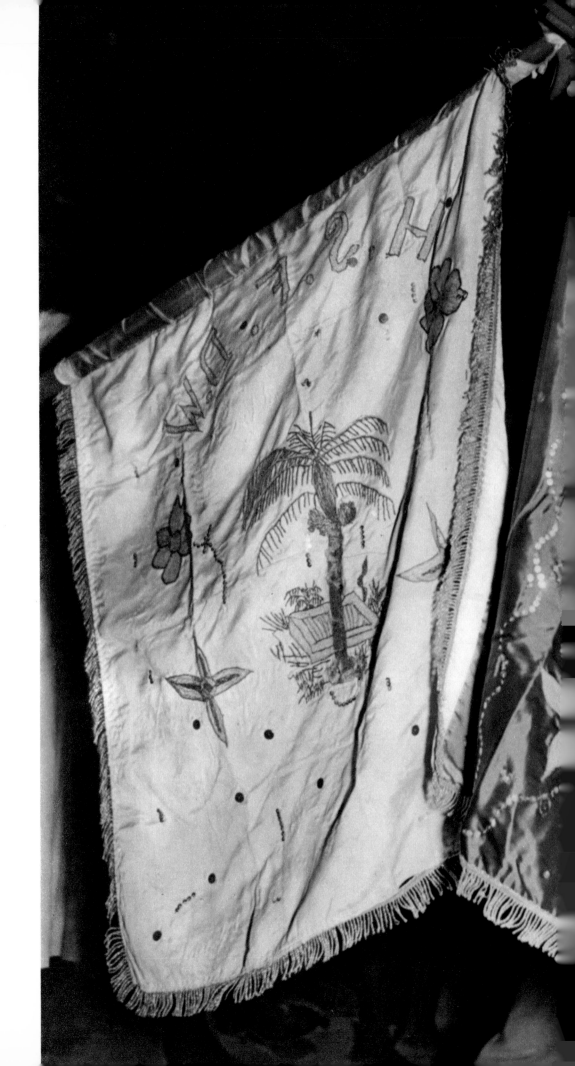

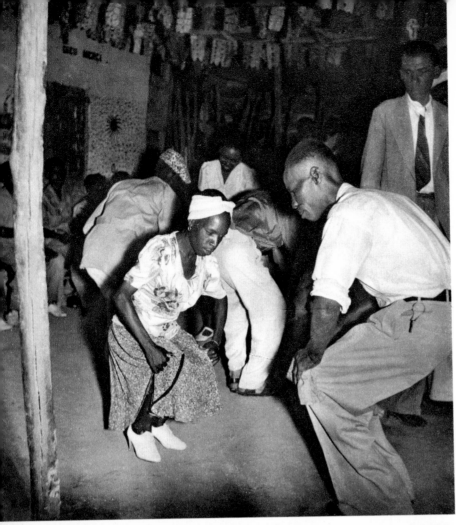

rather harshly. They are introduced by a man or woman holding a rattle, who acts as chorusleader, intoning the first verses which are then taken up by the "servants of the gods" in unison.

Since the spirits manifest their presence through people who act and speak for them, no statues or pictures are needed. Nevertheless, use is made during ceremonies of symbolic drawings, called *vèvè*. Depending on the sort of spirit to be represented, these designs are drawn on the ground with wheat or maize flour, crushed bricks, coffee grounds or ash. The officiating priest goes about it like this : he takes a pinch of powder or flour from a plate and lets it run between his index finger and his thumb to make a thin and even line. In this manner, he outlines geometric figures, objects or animals which may be on quite a large scale. Certain *vèvè*, composed of the symbols of a number of gods, extend the full length of the peristyle. Generally *vèvè* are disposed symmetrically around the *poteau-mitan*. If the *vèvè* originated from Dahomey, its style is decidedly European. The whorls and strapwork recall the patterns in wrought iron and embroidery fashionable in the 18th century. Despite stylization, one can easily distinguish the characteristic attributes of the *loa* : Ogu's sword, Agwé's boat, Damballah-wèdo's snake, Ezili's heart. The drawings give tangible shape to the presence of the deities and it is on them that offerings and the bodies of sacrificed animals are

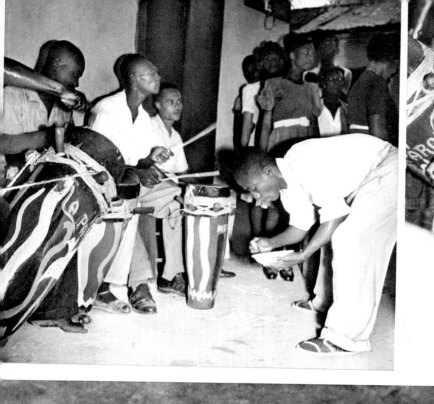

placed. They also possess the magic power of attracting the spirits. When a person possessed by Damballah climbs a tree and refuses to budge, the priest merely outlines a *vèvè* and the " snake-god " is soon attracted off his perch.

The ceremonies, or "services," of which voodoo worshippers must acquit themselves in order to find favor with the *loa* and have their sins forgiven them are known as "*manger-loa*", or "the feeding of the *loa*." The name underlines the importance attached to the food offerings made on such occasions. The gods are not addressed without being given a taste of their favorite dishes. Though the ritual meals are based on traditional Haitian recipes, the nature of the dishes, their preparation and the manner in which they are served, are all governed by rules it would be dangerous to break, for the *loa* are most sensitive in culinary matters.

The blood sacrifice is the culmination and climax of the long succession of rites included in every ceremony. At big feastings of the *loa* not only a considerable number of fowls but even billy goats and bulls are sacrificed. The bulls are covered with a silk or velvet mantle and wear a scarf tied at the roots of their horns as headgear. The color of these adornments symbolizes the god to whom the victim is dedicated. Those who persistently regard voodoo as a kind of witchcraft attach satanic significance to the lighted candles commonly fixed to the horns of goats. In point of fact, they merely emphasize the semi-divine nature of the victim. In voodoo practice, a candle or taper is lit every time there is communication with the spirits. The killing must be preceded by a rite which embraces both divination and communion. The victim must eat or drink a sacred kind of food or liquid. Refusal to do so indicates that the animal does not accept its own death and that it must be replaced by another one, since it fails to be acceptable to the gods. Those making the sacrifice try to establish as close a relationship as possible with their victim in order to identify themselves with it or infuse their own bodies with the mystic powers invested in it. The identification between sacrificer and victim goes so far that the former begins to behave as if he were himself to be immolated. He rails at his fate and pretends to be desperate. The faithful often bestride the animal before it is killed. Its blood is collected in a gourd and tasted by the officiating priest and the " servants of the gods " in turn. Some of the meat is consumed by the adepts, the rest being buried in a ditch or thrown to the four points of the compass. Writers short of sensational material have referred to human sacrifices and even to cannibalism in connection with voodoo. No such incident has ever been proven, and if ritual murders were once carried out, they were either committed by sorcerers or by persons acting at their instigation. Black magic certainly accounted for fewer crimes in Haiti than it did in Europe during the 18th and even the 19th centuries.

Voodoo should not be examined as a collection of beliefs and picturesque folklore. It is a religion of singular complexity which has lost none of its creative energy and " functions " in the technical, anthropological sense of that term. Voodoo is not only fervently believed in but its adherents never cease to enrich it with fresh liturgical or mythological contributions. It is ideal ground for those interested in the raw psychological impulses which produced our own familiar religions. The difference between a Haitian *houmfò* and a country temple in ancient Greece is not great. Nevertheless, one important difference between voodoo and the religion of other peoples and other epochs does exist. Voodoo belongs to the modern world and shares in its civilization. Its ritual language is contemporary and its deities have their being in our industrialized universe. Its beliefs and practices can be moving when they awaken memories of a distant yet familiar past. Despite the color of its adherents, it is a Western paganism to be discovered with joy or horror, according to one's disposition or upbringing. It is not Africa which must be sought in Haiti, but our own classical heritage. We can be enchanted by it in somewhat the same way as fairy stories transport us into a magical world without requiring us to give up our habits or break our links with the present.

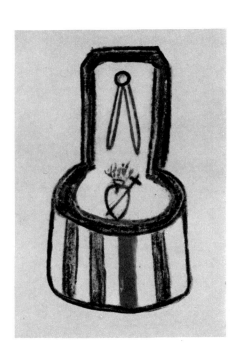

THE POSSESSED

Communication between men and gods is established by possession or trance, a phenomenon which is at once the most spectacular aspect of voodoo and its most disconcerting enigma. To the faithful, there is nothing puzzling about the *crise mystique*. It is nothing more than the descent of a god or spirit come to take possession of a chosen person after having dislodged one of his two souls.[1] The god uses the body of a man or a woman to manifest himself to his worshippers, share their amusements, make known his wishes or his will, wreak vengeance or express gratitude, as the case may be. Thus the possessed becomes not only the vessel of the god but also his instrument: in words and deeds, he conveys the god's personality, not his own. The play of his features, his movements and even the tone of his voice reflect the character of the god within him. The relationship established in this way between the man and the possessing god can be compared to that which unites a rider and his mount. For this reason, the possessed is called the " god's horse " (*choual*, in Creole) and a whole occult vocabulary is derived by analogy with horsemanship. One

[1] Every individual has two souls : the big and the small " bon ange " (good angel).

84

speaks of a god " mounting," " saddling " or " riding " a person and entreats him not to ill-treat his " mount."

Trembling and convulsions which are generally the first symptoms of possession are supposed to be caused by the displacement of the soul. The violence of such attacks naturally depends upon the god who is manifesting himself. If it is a boisterous deity, the shock of possession causes leaps and abrupt movements or riotous behavior, but the nature of this initial phase also depends upon the temperament of the possessed himself, who may react to an encroachment of his person by a secret force in various ways. If the possessed is not initiated and if his god is *bosal*, or untamed, the fit may be accompanied by spasmodic convulsions bordering on hysteria. Initiates of long standing, on the other hand, go into a quiet trance beginning with slight trembling and sometimes so gentle that inexperienced observers may not even detect it.

As a rule, the possessed appear to have lost control of their entire nervous system. Having been shaken by convulsions, they throw themselves forward as if shot by a spring, circle frenziedly, become rooted to the spot, their bodies bent forward, stagger, lurch about, recover, lose their balance again and finally fall to the ground in a half faint. Sometimes, such attacks start suddenly, while at others there may be warning symptoms such as a worried or distraught facial expression, slight trembling, gasping for breath, or beads of perspiration on the forehead. The features, in such cases, are puckered and pained.

The possessed are protected from the consequences of their own frenzy during a trance by the crowd around them. They are prevented from thrashing about furiously and, if they fall, arms are outstretched to catch them. Even modesty is preserved : women who roll around on the ground in a paroxysm are followed by other women who rearrange their disordered clothes. The sympathetic attitude of the crowd to the antics of the possessed undoubtedly engenders a sense of physical and moral security which enables him to abandon himself wholly to the trance.

The person "mounted" by a god loses his identity. So complete is the change in his personality that he refers to himself in the third person, as if he were a stranger to himself. He is at the mercy of the will and the whims of the supernatural being which is supposed to be in control of his body, and is naturally unpredictable in its behavior. The possessed, in short, is completely irresponsible and, in a way, derives no advantage from his close contact with the deity. When he comes out of the trance, he claims to remember nothing of what he did or said, and will stick by his assertions, even if he is obviously feigning. The possessed is told by others what has happened to him, and never shows the slightest sign of disbelief in this account of his own behavior. A woman whose dress was torn during possession came to ask me once how this accident—which seemed to worry her considerably—had occurred. Her pained surprise at my answer betokened the greatest sincerity.

Once the acute phase of the *crise mystique* is past, shoes, necklaces, rings or other objects which might be lost or broken are taken off the possessed. If there is trouble in keeping a real or simulated attack under control, a priest or priestess will come along with a rattle to calm the subject by shaking the instrument softly. The agitation of the possessed subsides gradually. Suddenly, a new personage appears : the god. His accessories are immediately brought along—hat, sword, cane, bottle, cigars—or, if he is to be attired in characteristic costume, the possessed is led to a room in the temple which is used as a dressing room.

Gods and spirits, whatever their own sex may be, manifest themselves impartially in either men or women. The possessed must signify, by means of clothes or behavior, the change which has been wrought in them. If the god which has descended happens to be Damballah, the snake-god, for example, the possessed darts his tongue, crawls sinuously along the ground, climbs the pillars of the temple or hangs upside down from the beams of the roof. Those possessed by the sea-god, Agwé, make guttural sounds to imitate waves and mime rowing movements sitting on a chair. The "horses" of Ogu, the god of war, don a French *képi* and a hussar's jacket. If they do not happen to own such military adornments, they tie scarves of the same color around their heads and arms. Ogus brandish a sword or a machete. They speak in clipped and energetic military accents, swear and blaspheme freely. They chew a cigar, demand rum and take long swigs of it while the chorus chants :

"Mèt' Ogou boué, li boué jâmê sou"
("Master Ogu drinks, he drinks but never gets drunk")

When a possessed, be it a man or a woman, appears in a silk dress, fingers heavy with jewelry and perfumed from head to foot, the onlookers know that Mistress Ezili is among them. The " goddess " walks slowly, swinging her hips, ogling men seductively and stopping for a kiss or a caress. Her whims are sometimes costly. She may require the beaten earth floor of the peristyle to be sprinkled with perfume. She treats women disdainfully and merely hooks her little finger into theirs. Since Ezili has worldly pretensions, the voodoo devotee who incarnates her makes an effort to speak French and talks in a high-pitched voice which is supposed to be refined. When Ezili returns to her boudoir on the arms of two admirers, the men rush to escort her.

There is a play-acting side to every *crise de possession* which is revealed in the first instance by the concern for dressing up. Such parallels between possession and dramatic performances, however, must not be allowed to obscure the fact that, in the eyes of the faithful, the possessed is not really an actor. He does not play a character, he *is* that character for the entire duration of the trance.

Nevertheless, one is tempted to describe as " theatrical " the performance spontaneously put on by the possessed when several deities manifest their presence simultaneously in different persons. The impromptu performances of differing kinds are highly appreciated by the audience, which shouts with laughter, interrupts the dialogue and noisily expresses its pleasure or discontent. Here is an example : an individual possessed by Zaka appears in the peristyle in the garb of a peasant. His wary gestures convey the uncertainty of a provincial who has come to town and is afraid of being robbed. At this point, another possessed appears—one might almost say that he " comes on." It is Guédé-nibo, of the Guédé family, which watches over the dead. Zaka is clearly terrified by the presence of his sinister brother and tries to propitiate him by offering him food and rum. Guédé plays the townsman and makes polite and bantering conversation. " What's in your bag ? " he asks and looks through it to examine its contents. Zaka, uneasy, cries " Stop ! stop ! " The bag is returned to him, but finally taken away while he is attending a sick man. Desperate, Zaka calls for playing cards and sea-shells in order to track the thief down by divination. " Play, Zaka, play," the audience chants. " I have come to complain about Agwé-wèdo," says Zaka. " Play, cousin, play." The objects called for are at length brought along.

Several persons are then suddenly possessed by Zaka and cause what in Haiti is so aptly called *youn escandale* (an uproar). One of them accuses a woman of having appropriated some things left in her care. Protests from the lady, general shouting, anger and invectives all round. Finally, Zaka is accused of the theft. His conscience is not clear and he gets worried whenever anybody goes near his precious bag.

The antics of the " gods " are watched with interest or amusement by the audience. People come up to speak to the god, who gives them advice or threatens them. If the god reproaches them for some shortcoming of which they feel themselves to be not guilty, their indignant protests are hardly held in check by respect.

These ritual trances pose a fundamental problem. Are they genuine cases of dissociation of personality comparable to those afflicting certain hysterics, or are they states of make believe which are part of a traditional cult and obey ritualistic imperatives? In other words, has a person who becomes the vessel of a god lost all sense of reality, or is he merely an actor playing a part? Those who have dealt with this phenomenon, particularly the psychiatrists, choose to class possession among the neuroses and make use of the term " hysteria " when discussing the possessed. It has been suggested that possessions occur mainly in persons whose heredity predisposes them to neurosis or hysteria. Such psychiatrists are misled by superficial analogies and neglect environmental factors. By pronouncing possessed voodoo adepts to be mentally ill, they gloss over the fact that, in peasant society, possession is a normal state and that trances are not only a part but an essential element of religious ritual. It is rather those who, believing in the *loa*, are never possessed who are the exceptions. Roger Bastide, the French sociologist, is also opposed to the definition of trances as hysterical. He points out that hysteria is a disease chiefly affecting whites, and that it is extremely rare if not actually unknown among Negroes. I have known a great many people who were subject to the *crise de possession* in Haiti, and none of them have ever shown signs of extreme nervousness, still less of neurosis in everyday life.

Nor is the explanation of trances in terms of collective delirium or orgiastic frenzy applicable to voodoo. Possessions do not occur in the middle of a crowd gripped by mystical fervor. Spectators chatting at the edge of the peristyle, smoking cigarettes and nibbling burnt almonds, are in no way contaminated by religious exaltation. The very dances, executed with an admirable sense of rhythm and much litheness, are not dionysian. They are more like difficult exercises to which one applies one's whole being, never allowing oneself to succumb to disorderly gestures. Ritual dictates that the gods be present at various times during the ceremony, and they never fail to turn up at the appropriate moment. Possession is therefore a controlled phenomenon obeying precise rules. It is considered to be unseemly for a god to " mount " a person who does not belong to the family giving the fête, and if he does so he is asked to go away. Similarly, every god is expected to appear in his turn when the devotees summon him by songs in his honor.

It is evident that the theatrical aspect of possession, which cannot be too strongly emphasized, is highly attractive to all those who have been disappointed and humiliated by real life. The very real satisfaction to be gained by a poor peasant woman who becomes the vessel of a god and is able to parade about in silken dresses acknowledging marks of respect from the crowd has not been sufficiently underlined by studies of possession as a phenomenon. What a release for repressed bitterness and imprisoned hatred! Since the possessed is not supposed to know what is going on around him, it is the god who talks through his lips and animates his body. The individual inhabited by the god is therefore not held accountable for his actions. Under cover of this alibi, he can do exactly as he pleases. It is also true that priests or priestesses promptly call to order a god who oversteps the sanctioned limits. There are numerous ways of mastering a god whose behavior becomes excessively improper or dangerous.

The *crise de possession* emits a power disturbingly contagious to unstable and nervous temperaments. That is why the sight of a possession sometimes causes others to break out, not only among the " servants of the gods " who are prepared to be " mounted," but also among those who have come along as visitors or out of sheer curiosity. In popular voodoo-practicing circles, a nervous attack is in no way shameful or disconcerting. It is neither inexplicable nor abnormal : on the contrary, it is a sign of divine favor. Exaltation and dizziness resulting from the frenzied agitation which precedes the climax create a mental climate favorable to a certain degree of auto-suggestion. Watching some of the possessed one is reminded of a child pretending to be a Red Indian or an animal and bolstering up the illusion by the use of costume or props. Adults help this daydream along by acquiescing in a certain amount of make believe and by using disguise to lend as much realism as possible. The possessed themselves are in an even more favorable position : the audience not only *pretends* to believe in their game, it really goes all the way to literal belief. The existence of the *loa* and their incarnations constitutes a popular article of faith. The possessed naturally share this conviction. The state of tension which follows a real or simulated nervous attack makes it hard to distinguish clearly between real personality and the character who has been represented. The possessed is an impromptu actor. The ease with which he slips into his part is proof to him —if proof were needed—that he has *become* a given character. He plays his role in good faith, honestly attributing it to the will of a god or spirit who, in a mysterious manner, has entered into him. In short, it would seem that belief in possession induces possessive behavior, quite without any intention to deceive.

SAUT D'EAU

The voodoo gods love to haunt springs and waterfalls. Near Ville-Bonheur, in the very heart of Haiti, the snake-god Damballah-wèdo and his wife Aïda-wèdo, the Rainbow, have chosen one of the country's finest waterfalls as their home. The river La Tombe, having crossed a green and smiling plateau, tumbles suddenly into space there. All the mysterious charm of the vanished forests of Haiti has been concentrated in the little wood which encloses the waterfall like a jewel case. Rainbow-hued haze rises from the foaming waters, deposits gleaming drops on the bracken and blurs the outlines of the rich foliage of the giant trees whose roots sunder the humid soil.

This oasis of coolness, where one experiences an agreeable sensation of lightness and well-being, is invaded by thousands of pilgrims round about the 15th July every year. As soon as they have arrived at the foot of the fall, the roaring of which drowns their prayers and their singing, they hurry to expose their bodies to the violence of the healing waters. They splash and jump about, excited, happy and awestruck in the knowledge that they are in the vicinity of their gods. From time to time, one of the bathers begins to tremble and lurches like a drunken man. His neighbors rush to his aid and prevent him from falling into the natural pool scooped out by the waters. The snake-god has manifested himself and "mounted" one of his worshippers. The attack never lasts long. The possessed makes for the bank, darting his tongue, his eyes screwed up, and giving forth small staccato noises. The adepts crowd around to talk to him, shake his hand and receive those many favors which the gods dispense to those they love.

A giant fig tree which grows near the waterfall is Damballah's "resting place." The pilgrims put small candles between its roots or suspend skeins of wool which they had tied around their hips from its branches. Everything is sacred, even the earth around the tree. Some collect a pinch of it and take it home in their handkerchiefs.

In Catholic Haiti, Damballah-wèdo and the water-gods cannot remain sole masters of so fine a waterfall. The *loa* have had to share their home with the Virgin and with St. John. Some miles from Saut d'Eau is the small town of Ville-Bonheur. It developed in the proximity of a coppice where our Lady of Mount Carmel once appeared at the top of a cabbage

palm. Healings followed this apparition and became more frequent until one day a curé, sensing idolatry, had the miracle palm felled. Since it was the roots of the tree which the believers worshipped, the priest had them pulled up, but they say the Virgin punished him for this sacrilege for he lost both legs in an accident. Popular piety proved to be stronger than the Church. Yielding to the faithful who came clamoring for the help of the Virgin and St. John, the clergy made the sacred wood into a place of pilgrimage. On the vigil of the feast of the Virgin of Saut d'Eau, garishly painted buses bring thousands of worshippers to the main square of Ville-Bonheur. They spend the night in the wood, which is lit up with thousands of candles. *Pères-savane* (bush priests) recite prayers, *docteurs-feuilles* (herb doctors) rub the sick with oil from lamps which have burned in front of the sacred trees and with water from the cascade, in which medicinal plants float.

In town, many pilgrims make merry, dance to a jazz band and converse in uninhibited terms with the prostitutes who have arrived in considerable numbers. Penitents, flaunting bright clothes in the colors of the gods they have offended, distribute food to the poor and hope to appease the African gods by this act of Christian charity.

The following day, the pilgrims who have gone to bathe at dawn under the waterfall, mill around the church erected in honor of the Virgin. After Mass, the statue of the Virgin of Saut d'Eau is attached to the roof of a lorry and paraded all round the square closely followed by a loudspeaker truck which pours out songs to the glory of the Virgin over the assembled multitudes. The faithful watch her pass with expressions of ecstasy and turn the palms of their hands towards her—a gesture made in Africa when a deity approaches a mortal.

94

SORCERY

Stories about zombies, which are very popular in Haiti, have greatly contributed towards giving voodoo its sinister reputation. Zombies are the living dead, or more accurately, persons who are considered to have died, who were buried within full view of all, but have been brought back to life by a sorcerer who has enslaved them. This resurrection is only partial. Zombies remain in a very dazed condition and are incapable of the exercise of will power. They resemble " those who have been given ether." They can be identified by their air of stupidity and their nasal voices. Their master locks them up in a room in his temple all day, and there they stay, mute and immobile. One of my Marbial friends claimed to have seen zombies with his own eyes at the home of a local *houngan*. He was not able to distinguish their features for they were sitting down with their heads between their hands, the very images of tiredness and dejection. At night, the sorcerer made them work in his fields, lashing them with a whip. The luckless beings groaned, but never raised a hand in revolt.

Zombies have to be fed, but care must be taken never to allow them a taste of salt. One grain is enough to dispel their lethargy and renew their will power. I was told in this connection that a Marbial *houngan* had transformed his mother-in-law and his own brother into zombies and locked them up in a hut on one of his plots of land. His wife, kept in ignorance of all this, nearly had a stroke when, happening to enter the hut, she found herself face to face with her supposedly deceased mother. Neighbors, hearing from her about the presence of zombies, secretly slipped salt to them. The zombies returned to a semblance of life and ran away, but not before burning their master's house and his harvest.

When the peasants suspect that the death of a loved one is not genuine, they fear that he will be snatched from the tomb and reduced to slavery. They prefer to forestall such a fate by " strangling " the corpse, or decapitating it. Thus sorcerers are prevented from reviving or exploiting victims. Many educated Haitians share the peasant's belief in zombies, but they account for the existence of these living corpses through the use of drugs known only to the *houngans*. Sometimes, flesh and blood zombies are exposed, but they are generally only idiots or lunatics.

The fear inspired by sorcerers who are able to change their prey into zombies is as nothing to the peasants' terror of a large group of evildoers called *zobop*, *bizâgo*, *galipot*, and also " hairless pigs," *vlanbindingues* and *voltigeurs*.

A *zobop* is one who, wanting to get rich quickly and without effort, has acquired a " burning charm " from a sorcerer. As a result of his intercourse with evil spirits such an individual loses all his scruples and acquires a taste for evil as such. *Zobops* form gangs and frequent country roads and paths after dark to attack solitary travelers whom they " eat," figuratively and sometimes even literally. Dressed in white and carrying candles on their heads, they march to drumbeats. Misfortune awaits anybody who comes across one of these sorcerers' processions : he is tied up with dried human entrails and sacrificed to the evil spirits served by the *zobops*. Others are eaten during hideous feasts or transformed into zombies. Among other things, the peasants accuse the *zobops* of changing their victims into animals for the slaughterhouse. Many are persuaded that there is a certain proportion of metamorphosed human beings among butchered beasts. I have often been told the story of the ox which knelt before the butcher and looked at him beseechingly the moment before he was to be felled. Changed human beings can be told from ordinary animals by their meek and sad looks. Many innocent people commit unwitting cannibalism as a result of these sorcerers' powers. It is true, however, that human flesh can always be recognized by a slight frothing and some trembling at the time it is slaughtered.

The *zobops* are quite up to date. They now operate in cars and " auto-*zobops* " are the source of fresh terrors. During my stay at Marbial, there was great fear of a ghost-car driving about at night with headlamps throwing a blue beam. One peasant even maintained that he had been kidnapped by the occupants of the car. At Port-au-Prince, the populace stood in great panic of a " tiger-car " which kidnapped children to eat them. I knew somebody who nearly came to grief on account of these jitters : one evening as he was about to get into his car which was parked along the curb, he was surrounded by a furious mob which accused him of being a sorcerer, the driver of the " tiger-car," and the kidnapper of a child which had failed to return home.

Peasants are quite prepared to believe that their very neighbors can transform themselves into animals and wander about the roads in this incarnation simply to frighten passers-by or to strike them dead by giving them a " seizure." Nearly all the country folk I knew assured me that, at one time or another during their lives, they had met a dog, an ass, a cow or a pig which betrayed its real nature by its suspect behavior.

Returning home late one night, a man from Marbial noticed a cow standing right across the road. He was convinced that there was something amiss about this encounter and that the animal was mysterious. Remembering that the whip he was carrying was "mounted "— that is to say, endowed with magic properties, he started to rain blows on the beast until he suddenly discovered that he was beating the chief of the rural constabulary. Crestfallen, the chief beseeched him not to mention the incident to anybody and explained that he merely wanted to amuse himself at the man's expense.

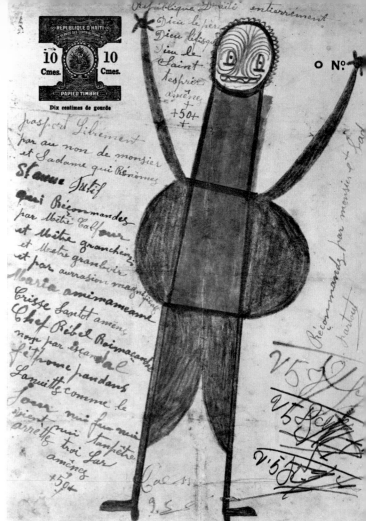

Werewolves, who are even more dreaded than the *zobops*, are feminine vampires who suck the blood of little children at nights. The werewolf preparing for one of these nocturnal sorties divests herself of her skin by rubbing her neck, her wrists and her ankles with an infusion of magic herbs and then hides it in a jar or some other secret cache where nobody can find it, burn it or smear it with red pepper. In her raw condition, the werewolf flaps her arms and legs to prepare herself for the flight she is about to begin. Flames gush from her armpits and her groin, and a turkey's wings sprout from her back. She rises into the air suddenly, right through the thatching of the roof. Luminous tracks—shooting stars, no doubt— mark her flight through the heavens. A law of the supernatural world stipulates that a vampire cannot eat a baby unless it has been offered to her by its own mother. The monsters therefore proceed in the following manner : a vampire, having alighted near a house where a

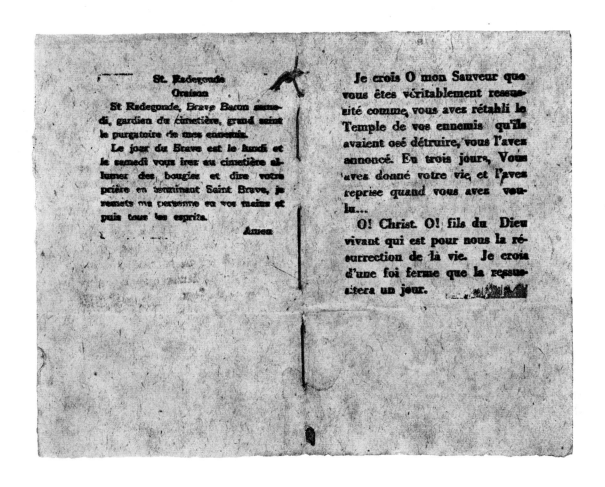

child lies sleeping, first enters the kitchen which, in the country, is a small shed at some distance from the house itself. From there, she softly calls both mother and child. The mother, only half awake, hears her name and answers "yes." "Will you give me your child?" the vampire asks. If the mother, drugged with sleep, then answers yes again, all is over and the child is lost. It is therefore the mother who clears the way for the vampire. In order to suck the child's blood, the vampire enters the house in the form of a cockroach or another kind of insect, or else inserts a long drinking straw between chinks in the wattle walls. Not all the blood is drunk at once, but the vampire returns every evening until the child dies, sucked completely dry.

The only way of protecting a child from vampires is to "spoil its blood" by bathing it in a solution of evil-smelling substances.

FUNERAL RITES

It would be difficult to exaggerate the importance of funeral rites to the Haitian peasant. None would hesitate to spend all his meager savings and even ruin himself to provide a fine funeral for a deceased kinsman. Though an element of vanity and a concern for " what the neighbors might say " enters into such extravagance, it is also motivated by deeper reasons. That the style of a funeral really decides the fate of the soul beyond the grave may not be fully believed or accorded a clear mode of expression, yet it does somehow appear to influence the behavior of peasants when face to face with death. In no other way can it be explained why certain persons are worried by the idea that there may be nobody to watch over their bodies, or that they might be buried in a roughly made coffin. That is also why the childless adopt children with the admitted aim of having somebody who will perform the last duties by them. I knew Marbial peasants who, as a precautionary measure, bought their own coffins and kept them carefully in their bedrooms.

As soon as the piercing and rhythmic cry announcing that a " *mortalité* " has occurred is heard, the news is relayed from hut to hut and soon the whole neighborhood is informed. Friends and relatives hurry along to keep the defunct company and make his last night on earth a happy one. Deathwatches are festivities eagerly awaited by young people avid for distraction and are greeted with joy.

Since the manner in which the watchers are received reflects upon the reputation of a household, the women, at their domestic chores, listen with only half an ear to words of sympathy addressed to them. They occupy themselves around large cauldrons in which water for coffee and ginger tea is boiling, or run to and fro between kitchen and arbor to serve everybody in order of precedence. From time to time, the closest relatives of the deceased, who apparently feel little grief, interrupt their work to lament the dead. Such lamentations consist of short sentences preceded by shrill and pathetic *way, ways* ; endearments are mingled with reproaches and references to a moving incident or other.

A few minutes later, the lamentations cease as suddenly as they began, and the weepers return to their task with serene faces, but if anything like the arrival of a coffin or of a friend of the deceased revives their grief, they start all over again. Relatives and friends relieve and " sustain " them, as they say, if they are forced into silence by exhaustion or the household chores.

Among the distractions provided at deathwatches, none is more curious than the chanting of the " *Marseilles*," an anthology of religious poems the full title of which is *Cantiques de l'âme dévote* (Canticles of the devout soul). It contains, in verse as inane as it is commonplace, interminable descriptions of the mysteries of the Faith, the lives of the saints and whole passages from the Scriptures. The voice being in key, the chorus would be quite bearable if some of the singers, throwing harmony to the winds, did not try to produce vocal effects which sound like brayings and which mingle with the buzz of conversation and the sound of clapping to raise a racket which is the more deafening the greater the honors to be paid to the deceased. Most of the men play at dominos or at a card game called three-seven or " wood-in-the-nose " after the penalty inflicted on the loser who must pinch his nose with a cleft bamboo stick. Those who prefer to gossip converse gaily with each other and do not trouble to spare the deceased in their jokes : " Have you noticed all the women who have turned up this evening ? Ha, ha ! that's because the dead man liked them so much."

Young people, in turn, organize games called *plaisirs* which, because of their association with death, assume almost ritualistic significance. There are acrobatic dances and trials of skill, little sketches on given themes and mimed scenes, sometimes touching on obscenity. Stories and riddles are also part of the *plaisirs* which make deathwatches so diverting. The stories are punctuated by refrains to be sung, which are taken up in chorus by all those present.

Burial takes place at dawn. The corpse, duly blessed by a *père-savane* (bush priest), is carried on the double and care is taken to turn and twist so that the soul cannot find its way back.

Every family has a cemetery in which to bury its dead. A big, black cross is generally erected, the symbol of Baron-Samedi or Baron-la-Croix, the Master of the Dead. Tombs are sometimes impressive. Over a century ago, Schœlcher already noted that " the ceme-

teries contain some most remarkable items, in very good taste and in the widest variety of shapes. Tombs are better built here than houses. Everywhere, even in the most wretched village without so much as a church or chapel, one is surprised to come across elaborate tombs, and it is quite usual to find them decorated with freshly picked flowers or, after sundown, to look through the gloom and see burning candles, which seem to have been lit by nocturnal spirits, so distant are they from any habitation." To erect a fine burial vault is a ritual imperative, the neglect of which may call down supernatural wrath.

After the final prayers, the soul—or at least one of the two souls every mortal possesses—spends a certain period of time under water. When it wishes to return to land, it makes its desires known by appearing to relatives in dreams. Should these omens from beyond the grave not suffice, the deceased strikes his relatives down with a disease of which they can only rid themselves by celebrating the *wèté mò nâ dlo* ceremony—fishing the dead out of the water. This ceremony is generally performed collectively, and for the benefit of the dead o several families. The priest shuts himself up in a tent, in which a vessel filled with water has been placed. Splashing is heard, followed by pitiful groans. The audience crowded outside can hear the dialogue between the priest and the soul of the deceased. The latter sometimes speaks to members of the family, reproaching them for their neglect or trying to console them. Souls thus rescued from the water are put into jars which are placed in the temple. Thus they become protecting spirits to watch over their family.

There exists a common fund of religious, social, moral and æsthetic traditions between the ancient Mediterranean civilizations and those which flourished along the Guinea coast, often hidden by conscious or unconscious racialism. When the whites and the blacks met in the New World, these spiritual ties acted, on the one hand, to help the assimilation of the blacks to the Western outlook and, on the other, to enrich white culture with numerous African elements. Though the culture born in this manner seems exotic, it is nevertheless within the general current of our tradition. Haiti is not a foreign land to us. In the peasants' huts, the voodoo temples and the drawing rooms of the élite one breathes a familiar atmosphere, not necessarily that of our day but compounded of images, words and attitudes which form a recognizable part of our own heritage. One must be grateful to Haiti for allowing us to experience, almost simultaneously, so many different epochs : Antiquity, the Middle Ages, the 18th century, the French Restoration and the American 20th century. Daniel Guérin, in his recent book, *Antilles décolonisées*, writes : " If, in the scale of material values, Haiti rates lowest among all the Antilles, in the scale of spiritual values it certainly holds first place. Contact with a people in rags, but brimming over with life, zest and personality gave me a feeling of joy which I never had elsewhere."

Revisiting the Marbial valley quite recently, I was somewhat disappointed to discover only too evident signs of a relapse into a state of affairs against which my colleagues and I had been fighting. I would have adjudged our efforts to have been a failure if a peasant, to whom I mentioned my disappointment, had not told me : " We learned nevertheless that, if we wish to better our standards of living, we must not turn to anybody for help. We must unite and work ourselves. The peasant must prepare his own salvation." These words mark a new spirit. In the whole of the Jérémie region, badly hit by a hurricane, I noticed the growth of sentiments the absence of which was formerly so worrying. The peasant seems to grasp his lot, and the methods appropriate for changing it. Rural communities are organizing themselves and undertaking collective action to break their isolation and make the best of their environment. All of Haitian society seems to be rapidly evolving, as is instanced by the middle classes' more flexible and understanding attitude towards the peasantry. The middle classes and the élite, hitherto composed mainly of mulattoes, are beginning to become accessible to blacks of common stock. Education has proved to be a powerful instrument of social mobility. Political consciousness has grown and a body of public opinion is emerging sufficiently influential to work changes in government. The future is certainly still obscure. Mention has been made of the dangers besetting the Haitian economy, but their very recognition and the will to combat them already constitute a victory. Haiti is entering a new phase in its history which will undoubtedly be characterized by hard work only. The day may not be far off when the wish expressed by Sonthonax, Commissioner of the French Republic, in the speech he made to the slaves whose emancipation, on August 19, 1793, he proclaimed at his own responsibility, will come true. It ran : " Liberty raises you from nothing to existence ; prove yourselves worthy of it. Renounce indolence and outlawry forever. *Show courage in your will to become a people, and soon you will be the equal of European nations.*"

PLATES

PLATES

PRINTED IN SWITZERLAND